LIFE ON THE MOVE

AN ANTHOLOGY

LISA WEBB

Published by Canadian Expat Mom

Copyright © 2019 Canadian Expat Mom

ISBN: 978-1-9993834-0-4

For my daughters, Océane and Elodie

Living on four different continents, you've shown me what it means to be adaptable, accepting, and brave. You've taken moving and travelling in stride since the day you were born, and you now walk through cultures with the comfort of true global citizens. You make me so proud to be your Mom. May you never lose the gifts you've received from being third culture kids.

A NOTE FROM THE EDITOR

Moving abroad can be the adventure of a lifetime, but it can come with unforeseen challenges as well. Sharing our stories makes us feel connected and less alone. In the pages of this book you'll find a sisterhood of strong women who, if you've lived internationally yourself, will leave you feeling like they've been there too.

The women in this book have brought forth stories of bravery, courage, embarrassment and straight-up humour. They've all walked into life in a foreign country and they're here to talk about it: the good *and* the bad.

If you enjoyed *Once Upon an Expat,* you'll love the stories you find in these pages just as much. As with the first anthology, you will find spelling conventions vary according to each author's favoured form of English, in order to hold true to the mix of voices.

Author royalties for this book are being donated to Mwana Villages, a grass-roots charity in Pointe Noire, Congo, that exists to serve vulnerable children and mothers through practical and sustainable ways, creating long-term solutions with a goal toward preserving the family. Learn more about Mwana Villages at www.mwanavillages.org.

TABLE OF CONTENTS

THE ITALIAN MOTHER-IN-LAW - JASMINE MAY-INNOCENTI

Italy is infamous for many things including bureaucracy and having little to no comprehension of timetables or the concept of line-ups, but I think there is nothing more infamous in Italy than The Mother-in-Law. In Italian, the word for mother-in-law is *suocera*, pronounced "swoh-chir-ah", and if you say it three times at midnight in front of a mirror, a perfectly-coiffed Italian woman pops out and starts criticizing you for folding the napkins wrongly. Jokes aside, the *suocera*, in Italian culture, sits upon her pedestal and is essentially untouchable, as she is, after all, *la mamma*. I should preface this story by saying that my mother-in-law is an absolutely lovely person; being from Abruzzo in Central Italy, she embodies the kind of warm and fuzzy feeling that you get when thinking about a plate of fresh pasta.

When I first met her, we did not speak the same language and it's likely she regarded me as more a passer-by than a soon-to-be permanent fixture in her life. This is in no part her fault, it has to do with the fact that I stayed with her one university Reading Week, just a month after her beloved only son, the prodigal *figlio maschio*, had returned to Italy after a semester studying abroad in Canada. It wasn't the greatest of first impressions. The airline had lost my luggage and so our very first interaction using gestures and Google Translate involved me asking her if I could borrow her underwear for the week. To be honest, I wasn't as mortified as I probably should have been because at a mere 20 years old, I had no intention of meeting my future mother-in-law anytime soon. In fact, I had humorously given my then-boyfriend (my now-husband) the nickname "The Italian" as I had never dated one before and my main objective in life was to be Carrie Bradshaw. Whenever he called me, "The Italian" would pop up on my phone, and I happily chatted to my girlfriends and mother about him without ever using his real name. This was how serious I was about the relationship at the time.

Fast-forward a few days past the meet cute with my mother-in-law; the reckless and sassy young adult in me decided to surprise my Italian while he was in the shower. It was midnight and I assumed his *mamma* and *papà* were fast asleep, based on the snoring I could hear across the wall in the guest room. In case you haven't already guessed, they were not asleep and we had a deliciously awkward run-in with this fact at breakfast the next morning. I just smiled and nodded and pretended not to listen as I occupied myself with my cappuccino, grateful to be exempt from the conversation due to my lack of Italian. Again, stupidly in retrospect, I brushed off this second *brutta figura* (bad impression), thinking I'd never see The Italian's parents again. How wrong I was.

2

Six whole years later, I would find myself with a diamond ring on my left hand and a one-way ticket to Italy in my right. I was about to become the foreign daughter-in-law to a woman whose underwear I had worn for one week and who had caught us being cheeky in the shower under her own roof. Finally the dread started to sink in. Those first few months, I tried to be on my very best behavior. We had a new house and I spent most of the time keeping it so clean and sparkling that you could lick the toilet seat cover and it would taste like Sicilian lemons. My Italian had greatly improved at this point and I could no longer fake a misunderstanding or resort to a goofy smile to smooth over conversations. Things were going swimmingly and I felt like I was regaining some of the family's good favor to make up for the previous encounters we had had. I wasn't yet working but was enjoying keeping house and on occasion, my mother-in-law would come over to keep me company.

As with most Italian parents, my future in-laws had been given the keys to our house, which comes with the unspoken rule that they can and will swing by whenever they please. I must stress that this rule is unspoken, because literally nobody spoke to me about it. I was under the impression that a quick phone call would be placed, especially since we were still in the phase of getting to know each other. Turns out that due to this unspoken rule, my future mother-in-law and I were about to get to know each other at a rather accelerated pace. It was my first full week in Italy after the official move when one morning I heard the key click into place downstairs. It was late, nearly midday, but I was still suffering from jet lag and the summer heat that made me extra groggy. We hadn't installed air-conditioning yet so as any woman home alone on a summer's day might do, I was comfortably lounging in bed in my birthday suit. *Click, clack, click, clack.* The sound of high heels came up the stairs. Before I could even process what was happening, the door of the bedroom swung open and I was officially up close and very personal with my Italian mother-in-law, in all my naked glory. No words were said; they weren't needed. There was very little that could get lost in translation from the horrified looks on both our faces. Needless to say, that was the last time my mother-in-law ever showed up unannounced.

Consequentially, we now enjoy the fruits of a rather intimate relationship, built on trust, understanding, and a shared traumatic experience. In fact, I wouldn't hesitate in the slightest if I had to borrow her underwear again.

2

AFRICA CALLS ME - CHERYL WALKER

I feel pulled between two worlds, two loves that I haven't figured out how to fit together. Over the years, I've struggled to find my true self in both places: Canada and Congo.

As I landed in Ethiopia on my way back to the Republic of Congo, in November 2016, the sight from above of the rough, earthy terrain brought back that light in my bones. I was connected to Africa. It had been eight months since I'd left Congo, after having lived there for a four-year stretch. This was the connection with Africa that I'd felt since my childhood, though I only set foot there for the first time in my early twenties.

We first moved to Congo in 2004, when my Congolese-born husband, Lambert, got a job in Pointe-Noire. We had met while he was studying in Montreal, where we married and soon started our family. For this move, we had packed everything we owned into a container and, with our three young sons in tow, set off for the land that I had dreamed about my whole life. However, the high of anticipation that I'd felt as we were preparing to move was quickly brought very low. Just one year after arriving in Congo with our full container and three children, we returned to Canada, with only travel bags, a few belongings and one more child on the way. It's true that that year was a failure, a disaster even. Everything that could go wrong did go wrong – we were robbed, I fell ill with malaria three times in six months, our son was hospitalized and our marriage almost fell apart – not to mention the culture shock and difficulty of living in such a different world.

But it wasn't long before Africa began calling me again. I first felt it about six months after we'd gotten back to Canada. Africa was in my bones. It was a feeling hard to explain to anyone who had not lived there and fallen in love with it. That year was hard for me socially in Canada, because I felt that no one understood me, even friends I had known for many years with whom I had previously had so much in common. It was a lonely time of soul-searching. Then, when I went back to Congo for a research trip, in 2009, in hopes of starting the charity, I remember sitting there looking up at the sky with papaya trees and mango trees on the horizon, and I noticed for the first time that I felt love for the place. This falling in love was what told me that was where I belonged. That was how I knew, and it is what gave me the strength and courage to face another move to such a difficult place to live, now with four children in tow.

In the Ethiopian airport, I can smell that I'm in my beloved Africa. The smell of people. Real smells. Urine and sweat. I don't really like it, but a part of me does. It's comforting and real, nothing masked. The washrooms are shipping containers with three stalls, with a black string to flush the toilet and a water bottle open on the counter with some pink liquid in it. Mosquitos are flying around me in the stall, and when I lean on the door that I had locked, it opens and I almost fall out of the stall with my pants down. I laugh. There is no wifi and the disconnectedness is refreshing and raw. I love the bare-bones simplicity. I feel free again – free and grounded to focus on what matters and not be pulled in every direction. My stomach begins to release its first-world knots.

I feel at one with the lady and the baby on her back, with the man wearing African cloth pants, with the people wearing sandals with the thick orange socks that were provided on the plane because it's surprisingly cold, with the man wearing the traditional hat and a white dress. We're all waiting together for the flight to my beloved Congo. We have a bond. We are in Africa. We are home.

When we decided to move to Pointe-Noire for the second time, in 2012, everyone was against it. They reminded me of all that we had lost the first time, eight years earlier. It was understandable that people thought we were crazy to do it again. But we saw it differently. The first time was a learning experience. Now we knew how to live in Africa, in a third world country. Now we knew what to bring. We knew to be careful about trusting people with our money, that people could be desperately opportunistic. We knew how to protect ourselves from diseases now. This time would be different. (Although who knew that I would soon become pregnant again, this time with twins!)

These were my reflections as I watched the movers pack up our home in the Montreal suburb of Pincourt. I watched them squeeze everything we owned like a three-dimensional puzzle into the 40-foot container parked on our driveway. They wasted no space. It took six weeks for our stuff to cross the ocean and another six to clear it from the port in Pointe-Noire. Meanwhile, I suffered through cooking outside on a charcoal fire, sleeping on my sister-in-law's old mattresses and trying to do homeschooling on a small plastic table in the sweltering heat while my husband was at work. I longed for my stuff. Living without a fridge changes everything about the way you live your life.

Having to buy groceries day by day, cooking on charcoal twice a day and many other things during that very hard time in my life made me realize what life is like for most Africans. They only buy what they need for today. This has a major effect on their mentality and outlook on life. They live in the present and don't plan much for the future. They are also very generous when someone is in need, to the point that they may share all they have today and have nothing for themselves tomorrow. It is because they are accustomed to only worrying about one day at a time. There is something to be said about that!

Moving back and forth to Congo, co[...] there, has really given me perspective on be[...] really don't matter. You can always get more stu[...] discovered that you don't really miss the stuff you think yo[...] miss when you leave it behind. Our things often hinder us from living our lives to the fullest. In 2011, the year before going back to Congo, I started to see our house in Canada as a big box that we were living in and living *for*. We were working so many hours to pay for it, and the stress of something going wrong with it was always in the back of our minds. The house took up a lot of my time because of all the housework it entailed and how much we had to work to pay for it and what goes along with having a house. Precious time. My precious life.

I had a destiny, a dream in my heart that I wasn't living out because I was so preoccupied with the everyday things in life. I could have entertained the thoughts that I'm too busy to do more and accepted that maybe I would never live my dream because life was in the way. But I knew that the menial tasks we do every day did not amount to life. It was just clutter. True life was doing what I was destined to do. I decided I would make changes and not let this clutter keep me from *living* my life. I didn't want to allow my belongings to become a comfort for me and especially not a factor in how I make decisions.

In 2010, we founded Mwana Villages as a registered charity with the goal to help vulnerable families, mostly orphans and abandoned children, with a focus on holistic care and family preservation. I didn't have it all planned out before starting and I didn't know what to expect or even what

just put one foot in front of the
be wise with the requests for help

ars, we were mainly helping children
ther or with a mother who had lost her
iildren in school and giving grants for
in the hopes that these women would
becon..   ient.

In 2014, e decided to open our Refuge for abandoned babies. The same week that our organization was approved and that we opened our doors, we were called to go receive two newborn baby girls. I named one of them Zola, which means *love* in Munukutuba. Zola was dark like ebony with long, thin limbs and fingers, beautiful, soft lips, and a strong nose. When I received her from the children's court, I fell in love. She was wearing a stained and ragged T-shirt that was much too big for her. She was tiny, weighing only about five pounds. As I walked to my car with her wrapped in my arms, I could feel her weightlessness and fragility. I climbed into the back seat of the car, staring at her beauty, like a mother who was blissfully seeing her baby for the first time. She was rooting for the breast, as newborns do, turning her head from side to side and opening her mouth wide and, since I was still nursing my twins and had milk, I instinctively gave her my breast. I was high with the maternal love I felt for this child I had just met whom I had not carried in my womb.

I called my husband at work and told him about her. I explained how her mother had thrown her away in the bathroom of a bar. I begged him for us to adopt her. He tried to be sensitive to my desire and stated the practical: "How will you manage with three breastfeeding babies... adopt them all, Cheryl..." and "How will you... you're too busy with seven children of your own?" ... was right. I have had to resist that temptation many times over the five years since we opened the Refuge. Every child is so precious and unique, and each one longs to be loved and to belong. We are thankful that we've been able to reunify some with their families and to have found awesome adoptive families for others.

When I think back to the decision to leave my comfort in Canada many years ago and what we gave up, and when I think about all the children who had no hope, whose lives are now full of joy and who now have the security of belonging, it makes me so grateful to have had the opportunity to leave my old life and do this.

These are things that never fade. Every face of every child will always be bright in my eyes and in my memory. Alongside, of course, my very own children, these children are gifts in my life and have added joy to my existence. Everything else fades – the hard-earned diplomas, the carefully-chosen furniture, the shiny new cars. It all fades or disintegrates. But the sense of having given someone hope, brought joy to their life, or shown them that they matter always remains, no matter where you are. You can bring these gifts with you everywhere because you carry them in your heart. They are what leave a true legacy after you're gone.

3

AI: FINDING MY INNER PEACE
_AND - STEPHANIE DUNCAN

Whenever those cold days in Canada get me down—the days where you step outside and your eyelashes instantly freeze in the below-zero temperature, the days where you anxiously wake up peering out the window to see if any sign of spring is visible—it's on those days that I take a deep breath, close my eyes and dream of a land that occupied two years of my life, my mind, my heart and my soul: Thailand. If I breathe in deeply enough, I can still smell the scents that tantalized my nose and my taste buds all those years ago: the salty smell of the Andaman Sea, the sharp aroma of spices, lemongrass, and fresh fish, and another smell that's not as easy to identify; the smell of adventure, independence, and soul-searching.

My two years living in Thailand often feel like a lifetime ago; that's because they practically were. It's been more than 17 years since my feet touched down on the island of Phuket, Thailand. I was 23 years old at the time and had just finished university in my home town of Toronto, Canada. Even at 23 I was admittedly wise beyond my years and knew that if I didn't leave home in search of the unknown then the mundane wheels of life would kick in; graduate school would be my next step, then full-time teaching and before I knew it I would wake up at 40 and wonder where the years had gone. I had an overwhelming urge to explore the world in search of a unique and exotic experience, something beyond the family trips I had done to Europe and the U.S. I knew I wanted something off the beaten track; and I knew that Thailand was just the place to get it.

So without a single connection to Thailand in my address book, but with a copy of the Lonely Planet and a backpack full of surf shorts, boho skirts and tank tops, I boarded a flight to Bangkok on October 12th 2001 (only four weeks after September 11; an event which added to my parents' anxiety), which would traverse halfway across the globe and take me to a place I was to call home for over two years.

I can still vividly remember the drive from the airport to the guest house I was to stay in until I secured a place of my own. The terrifying yet exhilarating way my taxi driver swerved in and out of traffic; dodging motorbikes left and right; passing market after market of stalls brightly displaying row upon row of exotic fruits and goods; the intense heat seeping into the taxi which intensified the boozy effects of a 27-hour flight and impending jetlag. I felt nauseated and clammy and could practically hear the thudding of my heart in my chest. Only one thought came to me at that particular moment: "What the hell have I gotten myself into?" My driver must have sensed my anxiety, and offered me a bottle of water. I gladly accepted it and returned his warm smile as I listened to him repeat a word that would become familiar in my new country: *sabai sabai*, meaning, it's alright, it's all good. And in that moment as I took a deep breath and looked out the window at the stunning scenery all around me, I knew everything would be.

My taxi driver would become one of many Thai friends and acquaintances I would make over the next two years, all of whom welcomed a *farang* like me with open arms. The Thai people are some of the most welcoming, laid-back people I have ever encountered. Perhaps, their Buddhist faith, which is deeply rooted in reincarnation, makes them so actively conscious of treating everyone with respect and love. After my first week there I could see why so many foreigners had decided to never leave the island; I could already feel the magnetic hold it could have on a person.

Living as an expatriate in Thailand entailed adopting the island mentality. Simple transactions like banking, postal services and government visas were not as efficient as the North American way I was used to. However, raising your voice and complaining in public was not the Thai way. And thus, after my first month I too noticed the change in my demeanour and attitude. Things that would have heightened my anxiety and made me paranoid in the past were now put to the back of my mind. I began to feel my shoulders relax, my tone of voice softened, and I was taking risks on a daily basis that I would never be able to drum up the courage to do now, as an almost 40-year-old.

I would often pinch myself to see if I was dreaming the life I was living. I secured a teaching job at a local ESL school. It would be my first experience teaching, something the school's director was not too concerned about during my interview, as she was too impressed with my North American accent and relieved that I had no distinct piercings or tattoos which would distract the students from learning. And so, with these qualifying traits I was offered a one-year contract with the possibility to extend it, four navy blue uniforms that I was expected to teach in at all government schools, and a very thin binder with the Dos and Don'ts of teaching in the Thai culture.

Now that I have taught in the Canadian system for over 13 years, I still fondly look back on those teaching days in Thailand. My Thai students were some of the best students I have ever taught. I miss the high esteem the teaching profession is afforded in Thailand, and seeing a class of over 40 students stand in unison to *wai* (bow with their hands placed in a prayer position) to me each time I entered the room. Foreign teachers were often treated like an anomaly and students might ask the ones who had fair skin and hair if they could touch these unfamiliar features. Parents were so grateful that their students had an opportunity to learn English from a native speaker that they would often ask us teachers to bear the responsibility of choosing an English name for their child. Realizing the weight of this responsibility I chose traditional names of family and relatives back home. Some of my colleagues knew this opportunity might not present itself again in the near future and decided to have some fun with the task at hand, naming the students after their favourite athletes and cars. I taught six boys named Beckham in one class!

Our teaching days were short and thus every late afternoon a handful of us expatriates who had formed an indescribable bond would head to our local beach, Nai Harn. We'd race there on our motorbikes enjoying some of the best coastal roads in the world as our backdrop. None of us drove cars as they were too costly, so motorbikes were our vehicles of choice. My first few months in Thailand were spent as a passenger on the back of one of these motorbikes, gripping on to the driver for dear life. We all had at least one 'Bali Burn' on our inner legs from dismounting the bike incorrectly, a trademark and rite of passage for every expat in Thailand. However, within months of driving the winding roads of Phuket our comfort levels would increase and with this so would our ability to perform certain tasks on our motorbikes. Sitting side-saddle in my work skirt, applying lipstick, smoking, balancing a surfboard or big screen TV, or driving my rescue dog to the beach, were all common occurrences.

My evenings, weekends and days off were spent savouring all that Thailand had to offer. I became accustomed to a lifestyle that I will probably never be able to indulge in again. I can proudly say that my accommodation (a two-bedroom, two-bathroom house with a lovely garden) didn't house an oven. Eating out in Thailand was so cheap and convenient that it was my preferred method and my daily routine would often consist of stopping at several roadside stalls for delectable dishes such as Som Tam (papaya salad with peanuts), BBQ chicken, sticky rice and the most amazing soups I'd ever tasted. My cravings for authentic Thai cuisine still often creep up on me, and in recent years with all 3 pregnancies my unborn child got a weekly spicy red curry in utero.

My friends and coworkers from South Africa, the UK,

Canada and America all felt like we were the 'real' cast members of the infamous Leonardo Di Caprio movie *The Beach*. We would jet set to go scuba-diving in the Philippines, trekking in northern Thailand, nightclubbing in Bangkok and full moon raving in Kho Pha Ngan whenever the opportunity would present itself.

I could have stayed there forever. But then after two and a half years my pragmatic self took over and I realized I had to move on. Months after my departure on Boxing Day 2004 I sat in my family's house glued to the television watching footage of the horrific tsunami that would devastate Southeast Asia. I watched the place I had called home be ravaged and destroyed by nature. The same beach where I took refuge every day for two years was practically wiped out and I knew had I been there my fate might have been similar. In the days that followed I frantically tried to contact friends and coworkers and heard harrowing tales of loss and death. I had toyed with the idea of going back that summer but the whole idea now seemed eerie to me, as if this magical kingdom that once occupied so much of my time and energy was something I had dreamt up.

But now, 15 years later and weeks away from turning 40, the desire to return is still as strong. I often walk into my local Thai restaurant and make an attempt to speak conversational Thai with the owners from Bangkok, just so I can cling to the little Thai I remember. My Canadian home (which now houses a husband and three kids) has physical remnants (bamboo candle holders, wooden photo frames) of my time in Thailand, and on lazy summer days I can still be seen in the yard wearing my almost awkward-looking Thai fisherman pants. Thailand was a country that gave me so much. It was the country that taught me how to relax and breathe (I did my first yoga class in Thailand and have practised yoga every week since). I taught my first class of students there and would go on to become a certified teacher. I fell in love with the culture, the landscape, the people and the person I was in Thailand.

So even on days like today, where I sit here with a to-do list as long as my arm and look out the window at the bleak winter sky, all I have to do is close my eyes for a second and I can practically feel the Thai sun on my face. I know I will return. This time when I do it will be with my husband and my three children, and chances are the experience will be a completely different adventure to the one I had when I was 23; but that's what life is all about, the adventure.

4

A BITTERSWEET JOURNEY - MONDI GALE KARVOUNIARIS

Born as an only child in South Africa in the 1980s, I feel like I had the best of both worlds. I grew up without technology, and my friends and I were free to roam the streets on our bicycles from a young age, yet we were still teenagers when the internet and cellphones made their appearance in the late 90s, so we were quick to adapt. I must admit I miss the carefree days before we were so connected. When boys first had to speak to your mom on the landline before they could speak to you. When we cared more about our next backyard adventure than our selfie on Facebook.

I was fortunate enough to grow up on a farm near a small town, in a province called the Free State. There was plenty of open space, a river right next to us, forests to explore, animals to tend to, endless adventures to be had with friends, and sometimes even my own adventures. I would run out the door in the morning and only come back if I was hungry, and my mom knew that I was safe and sound. I loved the freedom and that is exactly what I want for my daughter. I truly appreciated the childhood I had, despite the tragedy of losing my father when I was still young. At least I was able to get to know him and remember him, and my mother did an incredible job as a single mom, even enabling me to go to the best schools when we moved to Pretoria.

So, fast-forward more than twenty years and here I am living halfway across the world in Canada. I am here to build a life where my daughter can be free and where I hope to find my freedom again. A life free from anxiety and terrible fears, leaving behind a place with mostly beautiful happy memories but also horrific tragic memories. We left a beautiful country which has since been scarred by horrific violent crime and insurmountable government corruption. I am moving forward to something greater and better, a place where I can create my own happiness again and set an example for my daughter. So what led us to our fresh start?

This is the story of my journey.

At the end of my university studies I met Costa, who became the man of my dreams, with whom I spent nine incredible years. My true love and partner in life. We explored South Africa and were fortunate enough to explore other countries and continents too. We went on adventure after adventure. We married and lived in the house of our dreams where our beautiful daughter was born. Starting a family was to be our biggest adventure yet.

The adventure began in May 2015, the month our daughter was born, and with her, a dream for a new life and a new journey that we wanted to embark on as a family. Days after Nova-Mae was born, Costa and I decided we wanted more from life. We didn't want to run away from South

Africa; rather we wanted a new adventure, and to grow our family in a place we could live our purpose or discover what that purpose may be. We conducted weeks' worth of research regarding quality of life, environment, education, business opportunities, language and culture, and much more. Eventually we compared our lists, and on the top of both our lists was Canada.

There were many other contenders, like Holland, and even Austria, but the more we found out about Canada the more it seemed like an amazing place to venture into as we were approaching our 30s and growing our family. We loved what we had found out about the culture and the way of life, about the sense of community and beautiful landscapes. We built this dream in our hearts and in our minds of our kids running on the lawn of our little lake house with a backdrop of snowcapped mountains. We would trade our stress and anxieties about the political instability and violent crime, for 'first world problems'. We wanted to live simply and free. We knew it would be a challenge, but it was one we were ready for. We couldn't wait. We were so excited to begin the process. We booked our English test, the first step, and the very next day I was going to look for flights for us to take a trip to Canada. We were so excited. It was to be Nova-Mae's first international trip too.

On the 7th of August 2015 I was looking for flights with our ten-week-old daughter sleeping in my arms. Whilst researching, I received a phone call that changed the course of my life. My husband had been shot. He later died of his wounds in the hospital. He was shot for money he was carrying for his business, as that week they were moving their premises. I cannot begin to describe the grief and despair. That night as I tried to sleep next to our daughter, not believing what had happened, all I kept repeating in my head over and over was, *Lake house. Canada. Lake house. Canada.* Somehow, I survived that night and the days that followed. Despite the grief I still went and wrote the English test that September. I still hoped to fulfill the dream we had for raising our children in a beautiful and peaceful country. This dream of our lake house kept me distracted and helped me cope.

Three months later, with Nova-Mae almost five months old, we got on a plane and flew to America to stay with my best friend to try to heal. Nova-Mae was an amazing travel companion. Whilst in Ohio I met some amazing people. We traveled home just before Christmas and it was a trip that helped me deal with the loss and grief in more ways than one.

2016 was a blur. I won't lie. I don't remember much. I remember my beautiful daughter turning one, a number of children's parties, and meeting some incredible moms in the process, who are still my mom group today. I also remembered the lake house dream in Canada. Before I knew it Nova-Mae and I had visas and in December that year we flew to Canada. Again, she was an amazing travel companion, this time at 19 months old. We visited an old school friend and her family in Winnipeg and had a great time in the snow, learning about life in Canada. It seemed so natural. We ended up flying to Columbus, Ohio from Toronto in a twin prop plane. It was the tiniest international flight I had ever taken and rather nerve-wrecking and cold.

———————

Christmas came (I love Christmas in North America!) and then New Years went by, and I woke up one morning in January, in Cincinnati, knowing that I needed to move us to North America. The peace I felt in my heart was calming and serene. It was time to move forward. I returned home to South Africa and immediately checked whether the Canadian application that Costa and I had started was still valid. Fortunately, it was, but was set to expire in September 2017.

I submitted an application for Canada in May 2017, not expecting much, and after tons, I mean tons, of paperwork, Nova-Mae and I were accepted as residents by October. It all happened so naturally that it had to be divine. My house had already been sold in September and I had made contact with family I never even knew I had in Calgary. My mother received a multiple entry visa to both Canada and the USA. It was all coming together.

2018 then became a whirlwind of change. My mom and I packed up and sold the entire contents of just more than two households in two months. I packed up my car and a trailer, and three generations of women and three dogs drove down to the coast for a holiday. I no longer owned a house, or any furniture for that matter. I was free from so much clutter. It was liberating. Watching my dogs running on the beach with my daughter was also a dream come true. After our holiday we stayed with wonderful friends in Johannesburg, conducting final preparations for our move. We packed two suitcases each and in May 2018 all three of us got on a plane to fly one-way to our new lives.

"Welcome to Canada!" The large words we read were surrounded by hundreds of maple leaves, as my daughter, my mother and I walked down the arrivals passage in Calgary International Airport. It had been a 29-hour journey but we had made it to Calgary. We took the first few steps into our new lives, and almost everything we owned was in those six suitcases. (Full disclosure: there were a few trunks coming with sentimental items, and I still have a tiny storage unit filled with photo albums and typewriters.) We moved to a small town in Southern Alberta with gorgeous mountain views, and we began to settle in.

Living abroad was our dream and I am proud to have achieved it. There is so much I still want to give in my life, so much I still want to do, and so many places I still want to travel. I want my daughter to have freedom and choice and beauty all around her. Before Costa passed away, we had a wonderful life in South Africa but we desired more: the dream of our own little lake house with our daughter running to the water in summer laughing all the way; the dream of her playing in the snow in the winter and warming up around a fire drinking hot cocoa; the dream of camping and hiking in the great outdoors without fear or anxiety; the dream of growing and belonging in a place where anything is possible and we can truly be free.

I will continue to write our story and I will carry his memory into our new life.

Through all this my heart will never heal completely, but Costa's love for me and mine for him has enabled me to move forward and grow stronger. I now have new dreams and new hopes. I believe I can be happy again and I can teach my daughter, in turn, to make her own happiness. I am free again. I have the freedom I once felt galloping across a field on a horse as a child, the wind in my hair and adventure in front of me; the freedom to roam into the world and pursue my truth; freedom from anxiety and unnatural fear that has weighed me down for too long; freedom to raise my daughter the way Costa and I wanted to raise her; freedom to love deeply and share my words with the world.

Despite my new purpose and my new dreams, one dream still remains. I will watch our daughter play on the grass. I will watch her run toward the water. I will smile my forever bittersweet smile as I watch her laugh, joyful and free. I will thank the universe for leading me this far and for the adventure yet to come. I will breathe in the fresh air and be completely at peace, knowing that I am truly living and building a future despite the past. I will close my eyes and feel the wind on my face. And as I open my eyes and look up at the snowcapped mountains, I will whisper "Our dream came true," before I turn, a tear running down my cheek, and walk back into our lake house.

5

SYRIA - NINA HOBSON

Have you ever been on holiday and thought, to hell with it, I'm not going home?

The plan was to return to the UK via Lebanon. I'd been volunteering in Lebanon in a Palestinian refugee camp, and took a little holiday in Syria afterwards.

This was 2010 pre-civil-war Syria, a fairy-tale land where time and date didn't really seem to take hold. A land which welcomed young hippie travellers clutching *Lonely Planet* guides, religious pilgrims, and Middle Eastern businessmen in equal measure. A land where, after a couple of weeks holiday, the locals were greeting you by your first name and laying out your favourite *mezze* without you even ordering.

My bags were packed at the hostel, locked in the basement with those of my co-workers. My bags were ready, but I wasn't prepared to return to the rat race of London.

I took a last stroll around the hostel. I already knew my neighbourhood by heart: the dark, winding, so-small-you-had-to-walk-in-single-file alleyways which appeared to lead to a dead end, but then opened up to bright chapters of the bustling souk. I breathed in the freedom.

A little sign saying 'Beaty Parloor' caught my notice. Not because of the misspelling, but something endearingly captivating I couldn't pinpoint.

A gentle lady with a kind, round face was sitting in the corner, and she smiled when I stepped in. I didn't understand what she was saying, but she beckoned me over.

I'd get my legs waxed, I thought. I hadn't shaved, waxed or plucked in over two months and I thought it would be a good refresh before the journey home. I pointed to the hairs on my legs and made a ripping upward movement to mime a wax. Within minutes she was slathering the warm toffee-like gel on my shins.

Over my time in the camps in Lebanon I'd rehearsed a few conversation starters in Arabic. *Yes I love it here. It's a beautiful country. I love the mountains, the sea and the food. My favourite is falafel...* and so on.

We were chatting as much as my language skills and ability to cope with the pain of leg waxing would enable, then she asked if I was happy to go home. 'No,' I replied. How do you say in Arabic that your home is in the UK, that you're very content there, but you're just not ready for the Christmas sales in October, the *mind the gap, please mind the gap* underground train announcements, the crowds pushing you aside past the 'Keep Right!' noticeboards, the constant life goal schedules, the social media pop-up notifications, the LinkedIn emails reminding you that you still need to complete your profile?

'I have room. You sleep my house,' she said, pausing with the wax.

I took a moment to reflect. The call to prayer reverberated in the air with the scent of apple shisha from the restaurant next door.

'Yes,' I replied.

She smiled and packed up her tub of wax, moving over to the counter where she scribbled her telephone number on the back of an empty cosmetics packet. 'Dlall,' she said. Her name was Dlall; we shook hands.

There are no addresses as such in Syria, at least not for small homes in Damascus, so Dlall would meet me on the following Sunday outside the parlour and show me her home.

When Sunday came I met her at her shop and we walked in silence to her home. She was one of those people whose age you couldn't tell. Somewhere between 35 and 50, at a guess. Her eyes were creased at the edges from the sun and affectionate smiles, not from age.

She led me to a small alley beyond the main Omayyad Mosque and from there down a labyrinth of ever smaller side streets. After ten minutes of following her in silence, her footsteps hurried but with purpose, we arrived at a white gated door.

I stooped to avoid the low doorway. It wasn't beautiful in the conventional sense. There was paint cracking on the ceilings and a broken window. It wasn't chic, but it felt like a home. There were photos dotted around, pinned without frames to the walls, knick-knacks and keepsakes. This was a place of love and joy.

Dlall showed me to my potential room. There was no

bed, but she would arrange that in a week. I smiled and we shook hands.

From there my romance with Syria took hold. Dlall invited me to break fast after sunset at Ramadan with her family, to wander the market with her friends, for ice cream at the famous Bakdash cafe, to style my hair while Dabke beats sung out from a travel radio.

Her friends, a motley group, included a brash, endearing woman with crimson lips and tattooed eyebrows, a frail girl cloaked head to foot in traditional dress, whom I assumed was mute until she let out a few words of Arabic I did not understand, and an elegant, but determined mother.

I gazed around as this cluster of women whispered stories of the Mukhabarat, the secret service. I jumped in unison with them as the door gate rattled, and giggled just as loud to find it was just her near-deaf friend from across the market.

I'd enrolled in Arabic classes at the main Damascus university. However, feeling like I was speaking more American than Arabic, I switched to a mosque.

Abu Nour Mosque had been rumoured to brainwash its students into a radical Islamic lifestyle. But the fear of returning to the UK without experiencing a real slice of local life filled me with more dread than any supposed sect.

The day of enrollment Dlall helped me to fix my hijab over my hair and assuaged my fears that my abaya gown wasn't conservative enough. 'Very beautiful!' she shrieked as I did a little twirl. Dlall didn't wear a hijab. She loved God, she said, and this was all that mattered.

I arrived at Abu Nour and it was soon apparent that I had no reason to fear brainwashing. The teachers had given up on converting me, singling me out as the 'foreign' one, despite us all coming from abroad.

We were a mixed bunch — a Canadian mother accompanying her daughter so she could understand the 'real' Qu'ran, shy Eastern European girls whose innocent fresh faces made them appear even younger than their years, and homely Turkish women who insisted on feeding me during lessons, despite scolding from the mistress.

After many glorious months of trying to learn Arabic, I hadn't got very far. I couldn't chant from the Qu'ran like my classmates. I couldn't read traffic signs without squinting and guesses. But I knew my way around town without directions, I could cook a baked potato on a coal stove, and I knew how to make a flower tea to cure an upset stomach.

Living with Dlall, a gentle, but strong, single lady, I learnt the true meaning of female empowerment. As an atheist I saw the beauty in religion. I felt safe, content and free. I enjoyed a distanced perspective to put my life in order, to figure out my life goals without social media, advertising or well-meaning peers leading me astray. But Syria wasn't home; I couldn't expect the fairy tale to last, no matter how long I stayed.

I left Syria after my extended holiday, never to return. I often think of Dlall and I've tried via friends to check up on her, to little avail. I feel guilty that I haven't done more to find her and thankful that Syria was once a part of my life. I pray for her safety and happiness, as well as for the others who touched my life while I was there.

6

SPOTTED DICK PUDDING ANYONE? - MELISSA REYNOLDS

Motherhood comes with a lot of crappy jobs. There's diaper changing, midnight feedings, the terrible twos (and threes), the tween and teen years. I could go on and on. Being a parent comes with even more duties: vacuuming, dishes, laundry, after-school activity drop-offs and pick-ups.

Even though life is full of daily chores that need to be done, I would gladly do them ALL in exchange for the one I hate the most: grocery shopping.

I hated grocery shopping in my twenties, I hated it once I was married, and now that I have four offspring who all seem to live off different diets, I hate it even more. I study cookbooks and I even try to do meal preparation in advance. But no matter what, I am always frustrated and at a loss come dinner time.

So, I was already convinced that my first grocery shopping outing since moving to London, UK, in the summer of 2017, would be nothing short of arduous. The fact that it was in a foreign country didn't afford it any glamour in my mind.

Before we even began I was already at a disadvantage. If we had been at home, in our large house back in Toronto, with a full-size refrigerator and not one, but two freezers, I would have been able to buy however much I wanted. Costco and I were as tight as friends could be, and my husband and I loved stocking up on things at sale times. I did one big shopping at the beginning of the week and we had loads of food stocked away.

I sensed our grocery shopping was going to be changing. Our home here was a lot smaller; it had maybe five cupboards in total. Yes, five. And a half fridge and freezer. There was no hidden pantry, and there was no basement or garage for storage.

So this shopping list was going to have to be pared down, a lot, and for a few reasons. One, we simply had no space and two, I was travelling on foot. We did not have a car at this point and even if we did, let's just say that eighteen months after moving I'm still terrified to get behind the wheel and traverse the opposite side of the roadway.

And to top it all off: I had all four kids in tow, one in a stroller. (With good room for groceries underneath!) Let the experience begin.

I could see we were going to have an issue right off the bat. Package sizes are very different from Canada. Many of them are a lot smaller, again due to storage issues. Some packages of apples contain four. Some packages of muffins contain only two! My kids would devour that simply on the way home!

Because I was without a car, this wasn't too much of a hassle. There wasn't too much I could fit in under the stroller and we could only carry so many bags. But it was going to present a problem when my children ate everything we bought within a day and I would need to shop again. I was already inwardly groaning.

Next we went in search of eggs. Sounds simple, no?

After almost half an hour of slowly moving up and down the dairy aisles I was ready to admit defeat and was completely bewildered. *What kind of grocery store doesn't sell eggs?!*

My kids moaned and groaned but followed as I steamed off in irritation to find a store worker. Upon asking where the eggs would be, she quickly took me to the bread section. Yes, there sat the eggs I sought ON A SHELF WITH BREAD. The idea was inconceivable. Visions of rotten eggs from Halloweens of my youth, rotten because they had sat unrefrigerated, filled my mind. She had to be kidding.

"But they aren't cold!" I exclaimed to the poor worker. "They must have gone bad by now!"

"Oh, you must be American," she said with a smile. I let it pass this once. "Eggs are not refrigerated in stores here." Later at home I would Google that eggs in the UK are not washed and therefore are not required to be chilled, while North American eggs are sprayed with a chemical sanitizer.

Still staring in distress at the woman, I put the eggs in my basket. There was still a lot more store to conquer.

Fruits and vegetables proved to be a simple task. Bananas were bananas and grapes were grapes. Tomatoes were to-mah-toes; we were getting the hang of things.

Next we headed for meat. Now my kids aren't big meat eaters, but there are a few things they like. Among those, my son loves ham. Not the lunch meat kind, but a nice cooked ham for dinner. Simple, yes? No.

Just as with the famous search for eggs, we kept drifting around the meat department before I asked the nice butcher behind the counter. He pointed to the section so we headed over. However, all I could find were wrapped gammon joints. Immediately the words made me feel squeamish. Yet apparently this was our ham. While ham is already cooked and gammon is raw, this was as close as we were going to get.

Like most kids, mine love cookies. It was essential that we find cookies. We read the signs hanging above the aisles as we made our way through the store. Coffee, cereals, pasta...no cookies. Making our way through the different aisles one by one we found them—under the title of biscuits. Yet even under a different name, cookies are still cookies and my children were pleased by our eventual find.

Our shopping continued, finding nappies instead of diapers, chips instead of french fries, crisps instead of chips, ice lollies instead of popsicles and Sprite when we asked for lemonade. One of my children adores lemonade and it took a lot of searching to find one that wasn't fizzy. We were never able to find Kraft Dinner, but have made do a few times with Amazon delivery.

At the checkout the attendant greeted me, as she has for the past year and a half since, with, "Are you all right?" Now, I know most days I don't look my best, and I didn't that day, towing four unwilling children around the store. And yet she asks this every day, leading me to develop a complex about how truly dishevelled I looked every day.

Until I realized, only recently, this is a standard British

greeting that most people use. It means *how are you doing,* or *are you doing well?* My complex is still mostly there though.

This probably sounds like I hated London. And at first, I did. I was far from home, for the first time really, trying to adjust to a new way of living. I thought it would be simple; they speak English, we speak English, and it would be a breeze. But it wasn't. Every place is different and has a different way of doing things.

I have since come to love living abroad. Change isn't that hard when you have an open mind and I would like to say that our entire family has embraced our expat living.

Since living here for over a year I have become used to smaller packages and the lack of storage. You either shop more often (yay!) or you frequently have groceries delivered. I seem to do both. I get things like milk and fruits and vegetables delivered a few times during the week and make my husband take the car and stock up on other things on the weekend.

My husband helped even more by getting creative and making us a bit more cold storage. In the winter months we simply keep extras such as milk and yogurt in the trunk of our car. It stays nice and cold and that way we don't run out!

And I have tried to have a better perspective on my many grocery shopping trips through the weeks. I have obviously shopped continuously since living here, so things have definitely gotten easier. And there are still those few moments that make going to the store completely worthwhile.

Perusing the yogurt section one day looking for some my kids would eat, my eyes couldn't believe what they were seeing. Spotted Dick Pudding. I promptly started laughing and then, realizing that people were looking, grabbed some yogurt and moved on. But it was too good to resist. I doubled back and quickly snapped a picture for my friends. It is apparently a dough-like pudding with currants or raisins in it. Doesn't sound bad at all. But no, I have yet to eat some.

But I still giggle every time I pass by.

7

THE EVACUATION - CECILE DASH

"Cabin crew, please take your seats for take-off."

As we taxi to the runway I can't hold back my tears. I look around and see all my friends and their sleeping children, their crying babies, and I am not the only one who is having an emotional moment at this point...we made it, all of us....except for our partners and husbands who are left behind. We are being evacuated from the Republic of Congo. Our home.

We are on the only flight out that is still operating, at a ticket price which could buy you a small car; a flight that normally is run by mostly female staff, as Pointe-Noire is a popular destination for flight attendants since they get a 24-hour layover in the most expensive hotel in town...not this time though. This time the entire flight is operated by male staff who are not leaving the airport. *How long will we be gone? Will my husband be safe? Can we ever return?* I don't have the answers to these questions as we take off and as I watch my children fall asleep.

· · ·

8 hours earlier...

"And? What did they decide? What's going to happen?" My husband just got back into the house, the same house where we have been on lockdown for over a week.

"All the women and children are being evacuated on tonight's flight to Paris. You are allowed one suitcase per family and we will be picked up by an army convoy at 5.30pm."

"WHAT? Why are you not coming with us? But my sisters are supposed to come visit us in two days! One suit-case? When are we coming back? Where are we going? It's cold in Paris, we have no winter clothes! 5.30pm? You mean 5.30pm as in, three hours from now?"

How it all started...

We were all aware of the upcoming presidential elections which were due in the beginning of 2016, but nobody foresaw "the referendum". To summarize the situation: the current president was ending his second term and had reached both the age limit for presidential candidates and the two-term cap on successive terms. The first week of October we were hit by the news that the president had announced a so-called constitutional referendum to be held on the 25th of October 2015. The referendum, when voted in his favor, would mean that the current president could stay in parliament and serve an indefinite amount of terms. In a country as corrupt as the Republic of Congo, this referendum was just a façade. This was where the unrest started...

I had just finished an outdoor bootcamp with friends in

the Congo heat and humidity and was on my way back home when I received a message from a friend saying their company's security advisor had let them know to stay indoors for the rest of day, due to the announcement of the upcoming referendum. I phoned my husband to check and, in the meantime, started receiving more and more messages from friends to stay indoors as people were protesting and rallying all over town. After speaking to my husband, we decided that I would go and pick up the children, who were still at school. By the time I arrived at school my children were the only two left in the school; all the other children were already picked up. The drive home with my children, not knowing exactly what was going on, was surreal and scary, and my children didn't understand what was going on either.

In the next few days a lot happened: unrest, riots and protests getting closer and closer to where we lived. There were non-stop power cuts and our generator was almost out of diesel. Fuel shortages in town caused even more chaos as people were stocking up and preparing for the worst. The 1997 civil war in the Republic of Congo still left its marks and fears among the Congolese. Cellular networks were cut off by the government and our ways of communicating became harder and harder—we felt really isolated from the world. Supermarkets were running low on items and with no shipments coming in through the port, this was beginning to form a bigger problem. It was getting more difficult for our staff to come into work and most Congolese felt that this was their chance to finally stand up, and they would join the protests instead of coming to work. The army stepped in and made its presence aware all over town, which was intimidating to say the least. We heard rumors of people being harassed and threatened in their homes if they wouldn't vote in favor of the referendum. We heard and saw pictures of many people who died during these rallies and many cases of persons who simply vanished. These were mostly people supporting the opposition and thus not in favor of the referendum. Journalists were not allowed in the country and news was hard to receive, and when received, you couldn't be certain if it was the truth, or propaganda from the anti- or pro- referendum camps.

Al Jazeera: *Congolese rally against 'constitutional coup'.*
Al Jazeera: *Congo opposition protests turn violent.*
Reuters: *"People are demonstrating across the city. The police are firing tear gas bombs". Tresor Nzila, head of the Congolese Observatory of Human Rights.*
Reuters: *Thousands of protestors waved banners reading "Sassou get out" and "No to the referendum"*
BBC: *"Texting and internet services have been cut, there is a media blackout and public meetings have been banned ahead of a controversial referendum," according to residents*

Thankfully our internet ran through a satellite which made us one of the few households that still had limited access to the world. During this time, we had many locals as well as expat friends coming to our house or just sitting in our front yard to use our internet to communicate to family and friends that they were ok. My husband, being the warden for the Canadian embassy, was the only person feeding the Canadian government information as to what was happening on the ground. Cellular networks being cut formed the biggest problem, but in the heat of the moment it was yet another thing we just had to deal with. Thankfully we had one satellite phone in case of emergencies.

The lack of information, the unrest, the power cuts, the sound of helicopters flying over, the roadblocks, the fires, the sounds of the army all over town and the many lock-downs would make anyone feel scared. Most of us (expats) didn't personally feel threatened and understood the need for change in this country. Therefore we somewhat supported or were secretly rooting for the anti-referendum movement. But it was made clear to us upon entering this country to never ever get involved in politics or speak badly about politics. So, we didn't, and honestly, the only reason I am finally writing about our evacuation is because we no longer live in Congo. And what you are reading is the mild, very protected story of a person who was shielded from the actuality and harsh reality of what was going on because this is my story...an expat story.

For as long as we had lived there, I have been fascinated by the lampposts and the strings of rope attached to them. It took me a long time to figure out what that was about. Then I experienced a visit of the president coming into town for a few days, who brought along with him the explanation I was looking for. The entire city would be covered in pro-presidential slogans on big banners hung from...yes, rope in between the lampposts. So, then I started counting and from that moment on whenever I saw this, I counted the ropes as the amount of times that the president has made an appearance. To me it's a sign of the show they perform to impress the people, or the president, I am not sure which. Another thing that shocked me was that, prior to his arrival, busses would go into the poorest neighborhoods to recruit people. For a free t-shirt, a beer and 5000 CFA francs all they had to do was cheer on the president alongside the road. Which would then create a perfect opportunity to let press in to take pictures of all the people cheering on their president.

Breathe, be zen, breathe...everything will be ok!

We have three hours until pick up... let's start with putting our most valuable items in a suitcase. We brought everything to Congo...our entire life packed into a 40-foot container. When I say everything, I mean everything: wedding albums, children's photo albums...everything. Those items take priority over anything else. *What if we never return? We will lose everything...*I think about this and then come up with a plan: I get my phone out and room by room I go through our house; I take pictures of everything. I take pictures of the children's rooms, their beds, their books, their toys, their clothes, their stuffed animals, the bathrooms. I open kitchen drawers and cupboards and keep taking pictures. This entire exercise takes 30 minutes and almost 400 pictures later I am done. I feel relieved; it is just stuff and if we never return, I can show the kids pictures of all the stuff they had once owned, and we had to leave behind. It feels good, as if I just re-packed our 40-foot container in a more efficient way...onto the camera roll of my phone. Now, I have to make sure not to lose my phone!

It then takes us another hour or so to get organized and

fill up one suitcase, some hand luggage and an emergency backpack for my husband. The plan is that if things go bad, or worse than they already are, that the men will be evacuated by helicopter or boat to the nearest oil platform. I have completely switched to survival mode these past hours and everything seems surreal, until I look out of the window and reality hits me. I observe my guards who are sitting in the front yard still listening to the radio with intense looks on their faces. I'm sure they would rather be with their families then having to guard us for a salary that I consider hardly worthy of risking their lives. I feel bad that we are getting offered an out...they don't have an out and will have to deal with all the unknown fears and risks. Life is unfair! These guards, our guards: Emi, Armand, Jean Baptiste and Emar; our gardener, Fidel; our pool-guy, Jean; our beautiful maid, Christelle; they are not just employees. I consider them family.

"Mom, what's happening? Daddy says we are going on a trip?"

"Yes, baby, we are going on a little vacation. Daddy will stay here, but we will come back soon. We are going to Holland, would you like that? You can pack your backpack with some toys and snacks and I will come and check your bag in ten minutes, okay?"

After this conversation I go and lock myself in the bathroom and start to cry. I don't want to leave, I don't want to be in this situation. This wasn't in our expat contract...or was it? But did we just assume situations like this wouldn't happen to us and missed the section on evacuations?

"There should be enough food in the house as I stocked

43

up bigtime after the last lockdown, and there's plenty of water. There are two extra jerrycans with diesel as the generator is running low...are you going to be ok?"

"Yes, babe, I will be fine. Don't worry."

Sure, no need to worry, as we are being evacuated from a country that is politically very unstable. I would say there is plenty to worry about.

5.30pm, the convoy has arrived, and it feels intimidating. Some families are already on the busses as we enter but we still have a long list of pick-ups and the men are being separated from the women, as most men insisted on coming along since the route to the airport is not particularly safe. Driving through our neighborhood it feels surreal; this is OUR neighborhood and now we are going though it in an armed convoy. Thankfully the kids are distracted by seeing their friends on the bus and are excited by the prospect of all being on the same flight. The way to the airport is dark; as the power cuts continue it really is pitch-black outside and only a few huts along the road have a candle burning.

At the airport it is complete chaos, more so than normal. We are the lucky ones, the ones who have a ticket to get out. Not every company is evacuating their expats and I take this moment to think of all my friends who are staying behind with their children and hope that they will be ok. We go through to the check-in area; this is the part where we say our goodbyes. I look back at the row of men who are staying behind. That row includes my husband, my best friend, the father of my children; it feels so incredibly wrong, to be separated like this.

And then we are off...to the Western world where people

continue with their lives as if nothing happened, a world where Congo is hardly ever mentioned in the news. A completely different world. A world that doesn't feel like my world anymore.

The referendum was a façade that served its purpose with 92.96% votes in favor, turnout placed at 72.44%. A few months later the president was re-elected for his third presidential term. Most of the opposition disappeared or were arrested.

The experience taught us how quickly things can change in a country like this. We snapped out of our honeymoon period and began to see things the way they were. We were much more aware of the fact that this stability is constantly balancing on the edge. The first few weeks after being back "home" I felt scared at times and I think having been evacuated played a huge part in that fear. Being evacuated and returning without any new sources of information of what was happening "on the ground" made my mind go off and make things bigger then they probably were.

We are able to return to Congo a week and a half later when things are calmer, but still tense. The flight back to Pointe Noire leaves from Paris and as we wait to board, more and more friends show up. It feels like a family reunion, but so much more intense. We are being allowed back, but are still unsure what to expect when landing. We must be a strange sight, this large group of emotional people in the midst of Charles de Gaulle. Around us, people get ready to board flights to go on holiday or business trips...we are going home!

"Good morning, ladies and gentlemen. Welcome aboard this flight from Paris to Pointe Noire. We are almost finished boarding and estimated flight time is 7 hours and 55 minutes. Please sit back, and enjoy the flight."

To hear another take on the same experience, continue reading the next story, 'A Bag of What-If' by Catriona Turner.

8

A BAG OF WHAT-IF - CATRIONA TURNER

Packing an evacuation bag is an unsettling process. It brings absolute clarity. You pare everything down to the barest essentials able to be carried for a sustained period of time. If you have small children, you know it has to be a backpack, because you'll need your hands free to carry a child. If you have to carry those children through water, from beach, to dinghy, to supply boat, because, perhaps, the airport is already closed, you'll need to pack plenty of spare socks, and ideally spare shoes too. Even if you're in tropical Africa, you pack a jumper: a layer to keep you warm in case you land somewhere in the world where it's winter; a pillow in case you'll have to sleep without a bed. Towels, to dry, or act as blankets, or for more comfort on hard floors; a hat each, mosquito repellent, sunscreen, Immodium, paracetamol, sterilisation tablets. You have to remember the truly essential documents, like birth certificates, because you may never again see what isn't in those bags. You include as much water as you can carry and as many non-perishable snacks as will fit in the gaps, and make sure you can bear the weight for a prolonged periods.

Then you pull the drawstring, snap shut the plastic clasps, stow away in a wardrobe the bag of potential trauma through which you've just hypothetically lived, and return to your actual life. And there's a good chance it will stay there until some months later, when you're searching high and low for the birth certificate you need for a visa renewal.

I'm glad I'm not a survivalist. To exist constantly in that mindset somewhere between calm reality and worst-case scenario would be exhausting. I, on the other hand, enjoy life as a wilful optimist. I actually think it's what makes me good in a crisis: I won't imagine the worst, so I don't panic. And it makes something like envisaging considering a dramatic evacuation really rather exciting: a frisson of *what-if*, of *something could happen*, which doesn't actually bring real consequences.

But I did once pack an evacuation bag. And I did have to use it, just not for the *what-if* I'd envisaged.

It had only been a few weeks since we'd moved to Congo, so when October's *Toussaint* holiday approached, I was not remotely ready to look at another suitcase. It was an easy decision to stay put for the two weeks without school, even with the weary knowledge that the town would be even quieter and more sedate than usual. Our new lifestyle was already a fairly routine and constrained one, with less of the buzz and or diversity than we'd experienced in Africa before.

48

But this time I was willing to take on the quieter life to avoid a day of packing what we'd barely unpacked.

Most of our new friends were leaving town for the holidays, but a few others felt like us, that it was too soon after the long summer break. And there was a glimmer of something interesting, maybe even exciting, in the weeks that approached the holiday.

Ahead of a general election the following year, the president had called a referendum on the constitution, seeking to be allowed to stand for another term. There was likely to be protest, at least from younger generations; amongst older Congolese, the memories of civil war were fresh enough for them to live with the inevitability of the president continuing his now-34-year hold on power. I remembered a conversation with some Nigerian friends at the time of the Scottish referendum, and how impressed they were with our ability to be peaceful and civil about it. In many parts of Africa, political passions run high, and protests can escalate quickly.

So, maybe our Congo life was about to be a bit more exciting.

As it got closer to the last week of school, families started leaving, with many taking advantage of cheaper flight tickets before the holidays. There was some talk of others considering leaving, but the word coming from security experts was that there would be no need for evacuation; protests would be minimal, and confined to specific *quartiers*. Our company had been operating in the region for nearly 50 years, so we had confidence in the advice.

Still, there were default contingency plans in place that made for a dramatic mood. In the preceding weeks all the apartment buildings in the company's compounds had been fitted with extra security gates in the stairwell, completely blocking access if locked. Our own building held the company's crisis centre on the top floor, with its satellite communications equipment. Of the company's two main compounds, ours was the one further from any likely flashpoints, and right beside the coast, so would make for a better stronghold, if necessary.

On a couple of occasions we got messages to avoid the market or even downtown because of planned protests; nevertheless, employees were still able to cross town and get to the office. This was also around the time when we packed our evacuation bags, another requirement of the contingency plan.

However, as tensions rose, some of the smaller western companies in town took action. Without large compounds and extensive infrastructure, it was easier for them to remove family members from the country, rather than have to look after them in individual villas.

One Friday morning, after everyone was already at work, there was a knock on the door of families posted with an American company. Their security team had decided that, although the employees would stay and continue working, the families were to be evacuated. The flights had been booked for that very night.

I heard the stories afterwards (there was no time for last coffees or phone calls to friends) of rushed packing, and urgent requests for someone to look after the dog or cat. Families were suddenly having to put an ocean between them, with no timescale for returning, and no reassurances of how it would all turn out. There were tearful goodbyes at the chaotic airport, with couples wondering when they would see each other again, and, in the urgency of it all, imagining the worst.

Evacuation was not on the cards for us, however, so while a few more decided to take their holidays after all, those of us who were keen to avoid travel became the stoic optimists, sticking it out, too cool to panic.

About a week or so before the referendum, the SMS system stopped working, which in Africa is not only the most common form of communication, but also a popular way to pay bills, top up phone credit, and send money to family members. A technical fault was blamed, but the clear outcome was that organising protest became much harder. Then the internet went down, and the only way to communicate was with live phone calls.

So it took a couple of days before we learned that over at the other company compound, in a more central part of town, residents had been able to hear gunshots from a not-too-distant *quartier*. A few more decided to take their holidays, and good friends of ours over there found themselves with very few neighbours left. We offered to have them stay with us—a part of me relished the idea of bunking in with another family, finding the spirit of the blitz together, with no internet and just some board games and books for entertainment. But they wanted to avoid the upheaval to their family of five unless completely necessary.

It was late on a Thursday morning when the frissons of excitement turned to actual fight-or-flight adrenaline pulsing through my limbs.

Now we were midway through the school holidays, and I was chatting with some other mums while our kids played in the compound's play park. It was still the tail end of the dry season, so although the grass was grey, and puffs of dust rose with every pounding toddler footstep, it wasn't too hot to be out in the middle of the day. We were bored, and goodness knows we were probably complaining of having to do our own housework, what with the housekeepers and drivers quite reasonably keeping to their own *quartiers* during this unsettled time.

It was normal for cars to return to the compound in the middle of the day, for the long lunch break. But this was too early for lunch.

And it was different: a convoy of Fortuners and Hiluxes streamed into the compound, some peeling off to park in front of their respective buildings, the rest all nosing into the spaces in front of ours. A group of upper management and the security coordinators got out, and swiftly disappeared into the building and up to the crisis centre.

As my husband walked towards us from our car, I glanced back towards the compound's entrance. The gate was being shut. I heard myself let out a gasp, and my stomach flipped. I had never seen the gate shut before in daylight. I had never noticed its solid blank whiteness, the way it formed a continuous wall around the compound. We were in, and staying in.

Was this exciting enough, I asked myself?

More than enough.

The next day everyone was back at the office. I now know that the crisis point had come when a large crowd of protesters had been advancing closer and closer to the downtown area. There had been only about a dozen police officers to hold them back, and protect some of Congo's most influential business interests, but—by various means—they gained the upper hand. Protests continued afterwards in the *quartiers*, but the movement had peaked.

Back in our bubble, my need for excitement had peaked. I was honestly looking forward to the rest of the weekend, restricted by the *ville morte* curfew to stay in the compound, and able to have some quiet downtime as a family.

Saturday morning changed all that.

Our then 2-year-old, Ben, sat at the breakfast table, eating nothing. He was deflated. Our little joker held a pained expression, accented by tiny frown lines. When my husband put his hand on Ben's forehead he declared he was burning up, and that was when we noticed he was uncomfortable turning his head.

'Is your neck sore?' I asked, trying to keep my voice light. He nodded, winced, then burst into tears.

Being good in a crisis, I have been known to underestimate a threat, whereas my husband the pessimist would take our kids to the doctor at the first cough or degree of raised temperature. We've had many 'debates' when it comes to the requirement for medical intervention.

But this time, though, no debate was necessary.

We didn't even discuss who would take him. My husband knew that I was the one who could cope better waiting at home with our older son. He scooped up health book, car keys, and a change of nappies, and whisked our boy off to the company clinic through near-empty streets.

I definitely got the better end of that deal. I may be the one who watches closely as the needle draws a blood test, and is fascinated by fly-on-the-wall surgery footage, while he looks away squeamishly; but watching my wee boy endure a spinal tap to test for meningitis might have tested my stoicism too far. Luckily I didn't even know it was happening until after the fact, and my husband can't bring himself to relive it.

Meanwhile, at home, my optimism was certainly being challenged; even as I told myself that no news was good news, it was hard to keep still and focused on one thing at a time.

By the time I got a call, our worst fears of malaria and meningitis had been ruled out, and strong antibiotics were working to reduce the fever. But Ben was being admitted for further tests, and rehydration.

Half an hour later, having agreed with my husband that we would swap places, I opened the wardrobe and pulled out one of our backpacks of potential trauma. Although it was unlikely at this stage, Ben and I might still need it if we had to be evacuated from the clinic. I paused at the thought of leaving the other bag there in the apartment. The clinic was close to the compound, but still, those bags that had been packed together could be starting their journeys separately.

I undid the clasps and drawstring. There were new essentials to add. My friend on the other compound had heard our news, and called to offer help. She had one crucial piece of advice: 'Bring a plug-in.' It hadn't occurred to me before, but of course a hospital bed wouldn't have a mosquito net. Ben hadn't entered the clinic with malaria; I certainly didn't want him coming home with it.

When our neighbour dropped my older son and I off at the clinic, my world became very small, and very quiet, for the next 48 hours.

Half of our family went home late on Saturday afternoon, and as dusk fell, so did the curfew. Even with the expectation of recovery the following day, we would not be allowed to leave the clinic until Monday morning.

When I arrived in the room I found him half-asleep in the cot, unable to settle. It was an old-school raised hospital cot, high off the ground at treatment level, and surrounded by tall cage-like bars. He couldn't toss, turn or get comfortable without having to readjust for the IV tube trailing over the top of the bars from his hand to the drip stand. When he stirred and saw me, he raised his hand mournfully, to display the bulbous cotton-bud-shaped bandage his hand had become. 'They put a pipe into me,' he said, then lay back down for a fitful sleep.

There were more dressings, on his spine, as well as on his arm and fingers, where blood tests had been taken. The poet Norman MacCaig's description of 'glass fangs' came to mind, when I thought of how his vulnerable little body had been attacked by medical procedures.

He wore hospital-issue pyjamas that were far too big: collar up to his ears, ankles and cuffs turned up multiple times. It had the effect of diminishing him even more, turning our boisterous room-filling toddler into a tired and gloomy tiny person who couldn't even fill his clothes.

Later that first evening, the paediatrician was on his rounds with a group of medical staff. Ben was sitting on the room's bed by now, having woken up desperate to escape from his cage. But that was as far as his energy level had taken him; he wasn't ready to hear a story, play with a car, or even play games on my phone. His sporadic mewling cries were his only response to this unfamiliar sense of emptiness, of having a body drained of vigour.

And when the white coats came in the room, the cries turned to near-screams as he instinctively cowered away from them. The doctor explained that none of the tests had revealed the source of the infection, and that in ideal circumstances they would carry out more blood tests.

He smiled and sat by the bed, speaking gently to Ben, asking how he was feeling. He tried to take Ben's hand, to reassure him he wasn't there to do anything at that time. Ben's terrified reaction told him what he needed to know to make a decision. 'Well, we can see that the antibiotics are working to kill the infection. His fever is down. As long as that continues, we can just keep treating him. He is so young to keep having tests.' To this day, the source of the infection remains a mystery.

I remember that night as one of the longest of my life. Having been liberated from the restrictive cot, Ben was not interested in going back into it for any length of time, so he and I slept on the bed together. His sleep was fitful, mine non-existent. Every time he moved, this time we both had to make adjustments for the IV line. The book I'd brought was already finished, the only thing on TV was a French news channel, and without any internet, all the usual recourse for insomnia was unavailable.

The next day, however, although still pale and listless, he felt a bit better, and started to root in my bag. 'Want to play a game on your phone mummy.' When it was time to go to the toilet he walked ahead of me clutching his drip-stand. This time in his pyjamas he cut a comical little figure, pulling the drip stand behind him like some seasoned hospital veteran.

The doctor came back, and confirmed the all-clear, but that they might as well keep him on the drip for antibiotics and hydration, as long as we were there. It was a relief, of course, but knowing that we didn't need to be there made the next 24 hours or so stretch into infinity. Whenever Ben was napping I found myself peering out the high window into the ghostly street, craning for a better view, almost willing something to happen, wishing for some excitement...

But none came. Because, thank goodness, the excitement was over. The bags would soon be unpacked again, the essentials returned to their place in our still-new home.

And I wouldn't be asking *what-if* again for a long time.

Disclaimer: Sometimes our expat life in Congo felt like a reverse ghetto, our bubble a world apart from the real problems that people nearby were living. The referendum and accompanying protests in 2015 resulted in real problems, and real tragedy, for Congolese people. Simply Google 'Congo referendum 2015' to find out more.

9

THE FIRST CUT IS THE DEEPEST - LASAIRIONA MCMASTER

I've *always* wanted to be an expat.

Though, back when I was in school and dreaming of moving to America, I hadn't heard of the term 'expat'. I didn't even know it was a *thing*. I was young, and there really wasn't a trendy label attached to leaving home. It wasn't really seen as a positive, or good thing.

Back then, I was just a naive pre-teen in love with *The Mighty Ducks* movies (I knew every single word!) and utterly obsessed with the *Babysitters Club* books (I read them all, thrice). I spent my days lustfully wishing away the years till I was old enough to up sticks and move across the world to America, live off Oreos and Peanut Butter Cups, and find myself an NHL-er to marry and watch play hockey, Every. Single. Day. Back then, it was always America in my head.

At this point, I hadn't given any other country the time of day. There was absolutely no question in my mind that I would live in America—and I wasted no time in telling anyone who would listen the very same thing. All of my friends, and family, even the postwoman and the milkman, knew that *someday* Oliver's daughter from Parkhead was going to live in America.

It wasn't exactly the 'done thing' in the nineties. In the era of push-pops, crimped hair and the Spice Girls, people who moved away from home were certainly the exception to the rule, and *everyone* in the extended family (and all around the town) knew about the neighbour's cousin's wife's sister's daughter, Stacey, who lived in Australia, with no mind of returning to Ireland any time soon, if at all. Ever. It was almost a dirty word. A slight. Leaving.

'Can you believe it? SHE LEFT IRELAND,' they'd muse, agog. Like it was THE most heinous crime one could commit against the Emerald Isle.

No one really understood the mindset. 'You want to *LEAVE?*' 'It's just a phase, you'll grow out of it.' 'Sure, what do they have that we don't?' 'Are you too good for us?' The questions were endless. No one understood my itchy feet, my deep-seeded desire to become an expat. 'Do you hate it here THAT much?' they'd query. People who left 'The Island' were generally considered to be a bit snobby and up themselves, which in retrospect is pretty hilarious, because throughout my ten years abroad, that's not a word I'd use to describe many of the expats that I've met; they've largely been incredibly down to earth—and, I'd also like to think that I am anything but snobby and up myself (but for that you'd have to ask my friends!).

That's the reputation expats have.
It seems to be the reputation they've always had.

It'll likely be the reputation they *always* have.

But, in reality, you'll typically find us to be a wonderfully welcoming group of approachable, friendly, genuine women, who are stronger than any other human being you've ever known. In fact, some days I wonder if some of my friends truly are real-life superheroes and how the heck they manage to get so much done in a single day in a foreign country, while I drown in laundry and dirty dishes back 'home' on the Emerald Isle.

I met Colin at a hockey game. I told him on our first date that if he didn't want to move to America some day that we couldn't date and that was that. For real. First date—out with it, just like that. He replied that he'd just returned from a seven-year assignment in Houston, Texas, and that he was more than likely to return there within the coming five-year period.

Sold.

I ran home right away to order my wedding dress and book a flight to Texas.

KIDDING...

...mostly.

It wasn't five years later when we moved. It wasn't even three years later when we moved. I think, if I brush the decade of dust off my memory, we weren't even together two years before his company decided to move him back to Houston. We were 'just' boyfriend and girlfriend, we hadn't really talked much about marriage (imminently, anyways), I hadn't yet finished my college degree and I didn't know anything much about Houston. When we landed for our two week house-hunting, look-see trip, it was a day or so after hurricane Ike struck. I didn't know much about hurricanes either, and, with streets strewn with broken glass and dead birds, grocery stores cleared of every loaf of bread, bottle of milk and roll of toilet paper they had, and electricity being spotty at best unless places had a generator, I admit I had a moment of 'What did I sign up to, agreeing to move *here*?' This was only compounded by the fact that a few days later, we got stuck at the side of a major interstate in a carpark for seven hours because it flooded so badly, we couldn't move. I needed to pee epically badly (God bless a local paint store for opening their doors to those of us who were stranded) and my butt has only been more asleep on long-haul flights. I was miserable.

What was I *thinking*?

Was I mistaken to think that this place, this 'land of milk and honey' could be the awesome 'home' I'd imagined it to be?

It took six months (give or take) for me to acclimate to Houston. Six long, hard, tear-streaked, 'I made a mistake here', months. I've been gone from Houston for over two years and my heart still pines for home. I wasn't crazy. That foreign land deep in the heart of Texas? It became my home. During my seven and a half years in Houston, I got married, I made life-long friends (and, in a stroke of genius tied them to me forever by making them godparents to my child), I tried new things (I got my yellow belt in Krav Maga), I ate new things (If you haven't eaten from an H-Town food truck, you haven't lived), and I visited amazing cities across the country (I think New Orleans and San Diego were my favourites). I put down deep roots in the Lone Star State. I had fertility treatment, conceived, and, after waiting so long to have him, birthed my beautiful little Texan son.

Leaving Texas was hard.

Living in India was harder still.

Our eighteen-month assignment in Pune was trying. But, again, despite it feeling like an almost daily uphill battle, I wouldn't have traded the experience for anything else in the world. I met even more beautiful and brilliant people, saw even more amazing places (I'll never forget watching a sumo wrestling practice in Tokyo for as long as I live), avoided eating a lot of foods (man, they don't exaggerate that India loves its heat!), and enjoyed having multiple bathrooms and a lot more space than the three of us needed. I came away changed for the better, enriched by having lived there.

I'm technically a repat right now. My husband was made redundant a couple months ago and we repatriated from India back to the cold and dark winter shores of Ireland. I am struggling to find my sea legs again being back on The Island, not living the expat life surrounded by expat people, not having warm sunshine beating down on me when I step outside the door. But we are a strong breed, we are resilient, adaptable and enduring. We are capable, optimistic and determined. I will take this relocation just as I would have had we moved to another foreign land and I will make it my own.

My old friend Cindy used to say 'Bloom where you are planted'. It was her favourite quote; it's also what I remind myself when a new opportunity comes our way and our situation shifts from the comfortable and familiar, to the daunting and new. It's the perfect quote to apply to our transient lifestyle.

We are expats and we bloom where we are planted.

10

OUR DRIVER - KIMBERLY TREMBLAY

It was our first time living abroad when we landed in Malaysia. We were both nervous and excited for our adventure. However, after flying with our two young children for 18 hours, we were exhausted. Our arms were tired from carrying children, a stroller with two seats, two car seats, four carry-ons, a diaper bag and eight large pieces of luggage through the airports. We had to have two vans come get us to fit all our belongings and people.

Our assigned driver, Rosman, was a great help. He took our bags from our arms, loaded our things, directed the other driver, and welcomed us to his country with a great big smile even though it was late at night. The heat was thick with humidity and the smells were so distinctive and different from the cold, dry air we were coming from. On the ride back to our temporary residence, Rosman informed us he would be our driver for the next three months and we would see him Monday morning.

And so, we went to bed, waking early Saturday morning. Realizing we didn't have any food in the cupboards, we ordered a taxi online to take us to the nearby shopping mall. It was about a 15-minute wait, which in Malaysian time was nothing. Our cabby arrived and took us to a nearby grocer. Most of the grocery stores are located in the malls on the lowest floor. We walked around the mall for a while, trying to accustom our eyes, ears and noses to the strange surroundings. We stopped at the panda exhibition where we saw the number of wild pandas remaining in China represented by papier-mache ones on the floor. We stopped to take a photo and donate to the cause. We still have this photo. We look shell-shocked and incredibly tired, the four of us kneeling surrounded by miniature painted paper pandas.

We decided to head to the grocery store to collect the things that we needed to start a new life. Flour, eggs, fruits, meats, spices, etc, to get us through the next few weeks, were gathered, until the kids were starting to get antsy. We wanted to get another taxi right away, thinking there would be one out front of the mall. We waited and waited in the stifling heat with all of our food. Not one came by. Finally, after about half an hour of waiting and the kids thankfully falling asleep in their stroller after crying for quite some time, we saw one. I quickly ran over to grab it but some other expats told us it was theirs and we had to book one. We did not have phones at this time so there was no way to book! I was so frustrated and we both knew it was too far to walk. I found another taxi and offered double the price—no luck. I finally convinced a different taxi to take us after pleading for a few minutes about my tired children. By the time we got home, a lot of our groceries had spoiled as we had been out in the tropical heat for over an hour.

We quickly became aware of how important it was to have someone we could count on: Rosman became that person for us. We told him our story about the grocery store and the taxis and he offered to take us anywhere, anytime.

Over time we came to count on Rosman. He was there when we called. He helped take my kids and I to the school and pickup. He was reliable and helpful. And most importantly, he was trustworthy. After his three months, we decided to hire Rosman permanently as he became an important individual in our lives. We never thought we would have hired a driver but we realized the necessity for our situation and knew Rosman would help us if we needed someone.

My husband, Mat, would ride to and from work with him on a daily basis, discussing politics, religion and other pertinent subjects like soccer, which he enjoyed. On our daily trips, Rosman would teach me Bahasa Melayu (their native language), techniques for bargaining, and about his customs. He would often bring us local food from his mosque to try, as well as new fruits and local delights. We learnt about his culture as much as we could from him and he enjoyed sharing it with us. Mat and I would discuss our day with Rosman and how much we enjoyed his company.

We got to know each other better over the next two years. Rosman had a wife and four children of his own. He was a Malay man who loved his family and would speak with pride about each one of them. We would share stories on our long rides to town about our lives. Rosman became part of our family. He would show pictures of my family to his and vice versa. He would call my son his son, as his children were all girls. He kept us safe and was always a cautious driver, especially as traffic in Malaysia can be quite hectic.

I often would venture out into the city with my friends exploring the area, and its markets and shops. Rosman would drive us where we liked and would wait patiently until we were ready to go home. Malaysia wasn't always a safe place and my naivety was obvious to Rosman. He used to work for the army and the government as a bodyguard and was compelled to be mine. He told me one day coming back from one of my excursions, that he followed me through the market place and had done so a few times to ensure my safety. I was shocked! I had no clue he was there making sure I wasn't getting into any trouble. He was very protective of our family and made extra efforts to keep us safe.

One day when I was feeling ill, I asked Rosman to get my son from school without me. He responded without hesitation that he would, and would take my helper with him. While driving back, the car swerved and Rosman became too ill to drive. My helper drove the car to the nearest emergency room and called me immediately. She informed me Rosman couldn't breathe and had almost become unconscious. She then drove the car back to me and I came to the emergency room to aid Rosman.

I came in and Rosman allowed me to speak with his doctor. The doctor said he was fine, just to take it easy and go home. I had parked across the street and was walking Rosman out, when he collapsed. I quickly brought him back to the hospital and asked what was happening. The doctor took his blood sample and wiped a few drops across the counter. She attached the oxygen mask and left the room. I was extremely frustrated at this service. How could she let him go when he clearly was not ok? How could she wipe blood on the counter and leave it? And then proceed to leave a barely conscious patient in the room?

I became more and more enraged with the doctor as she did not return after a few minutes. I called out for her as Rosman's breathing became more delayed. She finally returned. I asked if he was having a heart attack or had a lung condition. She said she wasn't sure. I asked what tests she was running and she responded with, 'We can't run blood tests here as we don't have the equipment.' I was furious. This man who had taken care of me needed immediate help. I demanded an ambulance to leave to go to a more functional hospital, as I knew there was one parked outside. We waited 20 minutes for the drivers to come back from just being upstairs. They loaded Rosman into the ambulance and turned on the sirens. We went the wrong way down traffic-filled streets with the lights and sirens blaring. I was incredibly fearful. We only had to go 5 kilometers but it felt like a lifetime.

We arrived safely and they unloaded Rosman from the stretcher and brought him inside. Thankfully I knew one of the doctors there. He took Rosman's blood again, this time with gloves and proper care, and ran some tests. Rosman had a severe lung infection and a blood disease. All I could think about was how poorly the other doctor treated him; Rosman could have died, with his blood left out for someone else to contract this disease.

The doctor had the ambulance bring him to a larger

hospital and it took two weeks for him to recover under their care. The doctor informed me that Rosman was very lucky.

Rosman came back to work after his recovery time and he thanked me for my help. He shook my hand and began to cry. That was a first for us as Rosman was quite religious and did not have any physical contact with any women other than his immediate family. I knew that he had appreciated my help and support in getting him proper health care. Rosman came back to work and all was normal once again.

One evening, I received a call from Rosman's brother saying he was in a car accident. Rosman always rode his motorbike to and from our place. I thought he had had a little collision as that was fairly common there and his brother did not seem to allude to anything greater. He just said he probably wouldn't be in to work the next day. I asked him to keep us informed and let us know if we could do anything.

His brother called back in the morning. Rosman had been hit by a car which drove away. He had driven home to his wife even after the collision and was vomiting blood when he arrived. His wife quickly rushed him to the nearby hospital but, while in surgery, Rosman passed away.

We contacted his wife and family to send our condolences and a care package. We messaged back and forth for a while and eventually lost contact when we left Malaysia. We think of them often and see their Facebook posts keeping alive the memory of Rosman.

When we become expats, we often have to leave our own extended family behind. It can create a huge sense of loss and loneliness, which is why as expats, we tend to create strong familial-like bonds with others while away. That new bond helps us feel like we belong in the strange new environment, it helps us heal from leaving behind our homes, our friends and our family. It helps ease our transition from expatriate culture shock into adaptation, and even faster I have found when you have a local person explaining your new surroundings to you. They help you relate your homeland to your new home. They can expose you to different foods, areas of town, lifestyles and people you might never have known without them. You begin to experience a more authentic way of life rather than living in the expat bubble. Rosman was my tie to Malaysia. He was our guide, our bodyguard, and most importantly our good friend, and we miss him dearly. *Selamat tinggal*, Rosman.

11

A THIRD CULTURE KID IN DUBAI - LUCY CHOW

What is it like to live in Dubai? The UAE? Is it like the Sex in the City movie? These are common questions, and although I have never watched the movie, I have heard enough about it (the wild sandstorm that comes out of nowhere, and all the women needing to be covered) to be able to say with authority that life in Dubai was not portrayed accurately in that movie.

Dubai is definitely the most culturally diverse place we have ever lived. Expats from over 200 countries reside here. There's a mix of white- and blue-collar workers. Does every expat leave Dubai feeling like they've loved the experience? No, but that would be the same for any overseas posting.

I also get asked often about raising kids in Dubai. There is a normalcy to life in Dubai that people do not realize until they visit or live here. It wasn't until I visited my brother-in-law and his family in Las Vegas that I realized people lead the same lives there that everyone leads, once you are away from 'The Strip'. The same is true in Dubai.

Our son, Max, is 13 years old. He played in the Dubai Little League for five years and has been part of a Cub Scout and now Boy Scout troop for most of his life. Over the course of our time here, he has taken Mandarin, taekwondo, swimming, musical theatre and a whole host of other lessons. None of it really stuck, but suffice to say, the same myriad of after-school activities exists here, as elsewhere; all normal stuff.

Max calls Dubai home. He identifies with being Canadian, but has lived the majority of his life in the UAE. A wonderful example of the advantage of raising Third Culture Kids (TCK) came during the year of Canada's 150th birthday, in 2017. I had coincidentally met the Canadian Consulate General to Dubai and he was looking for initiatives to celebrate Canada in the UAE. While driving Max to school one day, I asked him how he would celebrate Canada's birthday in the UAE. At the time, Max was 11 and had been playing Minecraft since 2012.

He said, "I would build a world in Minecraft that has buildings from Canada and the UAE. Like the Burj Khalifa and the CN Tower!" Hence, an idea was born!

Essentially, Max created Community Days, where kids could come together and create in Minecraft. Three of these events were held in various schools in Dubai and one was held in Vancouver, on July 1 2017. His initiative was one of the favorites with the Canada150 Committee, organized by the Canadian Consulate. He had so much community support both in Dubai and back at home. He has various 'Canada150 UAE' worlds that were created at each event. This initiative did the following:

1. Shone a spotlight on Canada and the UAE. Students of all nationalities came together to build in Minecraft.

2. Created worlds celebrating UAE and Canadian architecture and locations, celebrating both countries through community building—literally!

3. Created a fun and educational opportunity for youth to participate in Canada150.

4. Shared the journey with Canadians and the world through video and social media.

Around 40,000 Canadian expatriates have made the UAE their home. The country is welcoming to all, irrespective of one's origin or religion; it is truly multicultural. The region has over 80 Tim Hortons stores, which is a famously popular coffee and donut chain from Canada. It has a strong Canadian Business Council, the Canada-UAE Business Council, as well as the Canada Club, which hosts more social events for the community. There is even a restaurant that serves great poutine, if you have a craving, and don't forget the indoor ski hill at Mall of Emirates, in case we miss winter. This extensive community means that Max was supported by many people along the way.

The kick-off event was really to test the waters. We managed to get space at in a tech startup space in Media City. The consulate and the Canadian Chamber spread the word. The response was overwhelming. On the day, there was standing room only for parents. Furthermore, the Consulate overwhelmed us by sending two visiting Royal Canadian Mounted Police officers in their recognizable Red

Serge jackets to provide a 'meet and greet' for the attendees! These were the same officers that were present at the Bryan Adams concert in Dubai, all part of the Canada150 festivities. Honestly, I had seen RCMP officers in parades and from afar, but up close, they are even more impressive. How ironic that I had to move all the way to Dubai to meet RCMP officers. I was thrilled that they were both female officers and mothers themselves. They loved Max's initiative! There were kids from seven years old and upwards, girls and boys, from all nationalities. Over 50 kids came out to participate. Max presented a brief overview and the kids all logged into a server that Max set up for the event. He had printed forms with ideas of buildings from the UAE and Canada that kids could build. The 'world' soon became populated. Kids worked in teams if they wanted to, and many did. At the end of four hours the world contained more than 40 buildings from both countries, everything from a sophisticated ice rink from Canada, to the Dubai Mall Aquarium! They built an amazing world filled with the Burj Al Arab, Calgary Stampede grounds and much more.

After holding a few events in Dubai, I thought it would be amazing if Max could hold a Community Day back in Vancouver, where we travel home every summer. The Consulate of Canada in Dubai connected us to their counterparts back home. We found a venue and a spokesperson, and were given Canada150 flags and tattoos to hand out. On Canada Day, July 1 2017, Max opened his Canada150 UAE Community Day in Vancouver: my home, the place where I was born and raised. My family all came out to support him. It was surreal in a way. Max was born in Hong Kong, when my husband, Ray, and I were expats there, then he lived 10 years of his life in Dubai. It was clear that things had come full circle and it was so amazing to see that people in Vancouver cared that this kid from the UAE was holding this Community Day. The world can be a small place and Max was fortunate to have found support for his initiative in Dubai *and* Canada. I know Max understood it was great for him to have held his event in Canada. But the full significance will probably be lost on him until he is a bit older.

The fact that this idea was initiated by an 11-year-old Canadian, living in Dubai, is a testament to the benefits of raising TCKs! 'Youth' was one of the pillars of Canada150. Max is an example of how awesome kids of his generation are. If you ask him today about Minecraft, he will say he has moved on from that platform. But Canada150 UAE created a sense of community for many of the kids and families who participated. It provided face-to-face collaborative opportunities that lasted beyond celebrating Canada's birthday. There is a real concern that our kids are interacting more and more online. Whether you live in Seattle, Beijing, or Dubai, all parents wring their hands over the same issues. Kids live on the internet, social media, and watch shows on their phones. Getting out, meeting other people, and creating through Canada150 UAE allowed magic to happen. Technology does not have to be all bad. How can the platform be utilized creatively? How can tech be used to bring people together, instead of alienating them?

Being brought up as a third culture kid, Max's comfort in bridging cultures comes naturally. Thomas Speckhardt is Executive Director of YouthCompass International and he says that TCKs are natural bridge-builders who have the ability to understand and operate in different cultures and that they're perfectly situated for international business and politics.

In the end, maybe our most important job as parents of TCKs isn't to help them find a spot on the map to call home, but rather to help them embrace their membership in a community of global nomads who all belong to each other.

12

A BEAUTIFUL MESS - AMANDA HEIN

You are so brave! How can you just do that? What if it doesn't work out like you expected? Aren't you scared to leave? How will you be able to speak with the people there? And what about work? And making friends?!... I had heard it all after I spontaneously quit my job in Canada and moved to Germany. Was I unsure? Definitely! I was moving to a country where I couldn't speak the language and knew one person – my nearly-10-years-younger boyfriend whom I had known only six months. I was planning to move in with his family. It was a ridiculous plan but I craved the unknown and risk of it all. Five years later, I am still riding this roller coaster of a beautiful mess!

After being in Germany only a few weeks, I heard that my boyfriend was cheating on me. It was a slap in the face and I was devastated. I had just left everyone and everything behind to move across the world to be with this person I thought I really loved, and now I heard he was cheating on me. I felt like a fool so I confronted him. Obviously he denied it and so I believed him. I badly wanted this whole adventure to work out. I wanted to learn the language and work in Germany. I wanted to meet friends and grow some roots. I wanted to show my parents I could handle this on my own and that I made the right decision coming here in the first place. So I turned a blind eye and ended up living in a messy misery.

It was an awful time. The lowest in my life. I was alone in a country with none of my `Canadian´ people. My now ex-boyfriend constantly threatened me with the fact that I had nowhere to go. That I knew no one. He would ask me how I planned to leave him. I had no money as I was still in the process of obtaining my working visa. He played on that, and on the fact that I was so new to the country, what could I do? He made me feel helpless. Sure I had made some friends but did I really plan to move in with them? It just wasn't that easy. I was at the very bottom of the bottom. I failed. I failed myself. I failed my parents by leaving Canada. I failed my relationship. I was just a huge failure. Or so I felt at the time.

One evening in the midst of this mess I drove myself to a bench that overlooks a valley. I will never forget that day. I sat and watched the sunset. I thought of the ways I could finally just end everything—my life. I truly considered it, down to the details. It was a hard time. A very hard time. Being away from home and feeling so alone, it was like I was broken. There was a black cloud that followed my every single move. But the longer I sat on that bench, the longer I just felt that I couldn't bring myself to do it and am I ever glad I made the decision not to! Instead I drove home and cried myself to sleep like I had done for months.

After nearly three long years of this toxic relationship, I was done. I ended it for good. I had finally caught him and there were no more lies he could hide behind. It was all out now. I knew everything and it was over. I was finally in a much better place, away from the toxicity. I was making money and could speak German almost fluently. I had my own apartment and some really great friends. I had people who had gone out of their way to help me and who were there for me through the awful, dark days. I will forever be thankful for them and everything they did for me. It's crazy just how important some people can become in such a short time. I have learned through all of these hard times that true friendship isn't based on how many years you have known someone, but rather, who is there for you when you need them the most.

Fast forward many awkward moments, what seemed like never-ending struggles, feelings of constant miscommunications, absolute loneliness, homesickness, and everything else living overseas brings, to this present moment in time. I am happily married to an amazing German man. He has shown me the true meaning of real love, kindness, compassion, patience, caring, and respect. There are still moments of miscommunication, which there probably always will be but hey, that's life. There are still struggles and awkward moments, but where in the world aren't there struggles and who isn't awkward from time to time? The homesickness will always come and go but the loneliness has been filled with having the most heart-warming, beautiful person by my side.

I now have two homes, 7000 kilometers apart. This is my reality. I have two places where I have loved ones. I have two places where I feel like myself. In both places I am happy, I know the language, and how to get around. I know the different foods and traditions, and in both places I have good friends I can call up anytime to come over and visit. But in the end I can't split myself. I just know, no matter where I am, Canada or Germany, I am loved and wanted, and that is by far the best feeling of home anyone can ask for. What may have been for many years a messy misery truly turned out to be my beautiful mess.

13

TURNING BACK TIME...AND A NEW BEGINNING - SANDRA GLUECK-TAGLIEBER

These first days in the new year have me feeling a bit sentimental as I realize it has been 14 years, covering almost my whole adult life, since I jumped on a roller coaster ride that would consistently challenge me, both personally and professionally. And it is also hard to imagine that our globetrotting, pathfinding journey will be over in the summer. The plan for 2019 includes resettling "home" in Austria, though plans might change, as we all know. But let me turn back time and start at the beginning.

Back in 2004, a fresh graduate from university, I was selected amongst five other people for a special trainee program in Austria focusing on a career in the institutions of the European Union. As you can imagine, this was quite an achievement, and a career opportunity one would not throw away easily. I had had the same boyfriend for years and everyone around us, including us, could see us having a house and kids near our hometown within a couple of years.

And then, out of the blue, along came this man who

simply seemed to be "the one" for me. He was in a similar trainee program in Austria but one which foresaw a diplomatic career with frequent changes of destination: every three years initially, and later a frequency of five to seven years. Honestly, I did not spend much time thinking about what his career would mean for me and my future, when I embarked on my expat spouse journey shortly after New Year 2005. I had just decided, naïvely or not, to follow my gut and go with him wherever he would go or be sent. It was a decision which I had made all by myself, ignoring all thoughts and input from my family and friends, probably afraid I would lose my courage.

Abu Dhabi, Zagreb, Montreal, Brussels: 14 years later and having lived, worked and travelled all around the globe, having tied the knot with the love of my life, and given birth to our most wonderful little man in Belgium, I have probably seen almost every expat spouse set-up imaginable: unemployed; employed; founding, managing and selling a private limited company; self-employed; freelancing; volunteering (a lot!); becoming a mum; becoming a mompreneur. I've discovered that there are always possibilities.

If I could turn back time, would I change my decision? My heartfelt answer is, no! Okay, I admit, on bad days I would probably say I was, or perhaps *am*, crazy and naïve, having given up a lot; but on the good days, and thankfully there are more of those, I do not regret our nomadic journey. I would jump on that very first plane again any time.

However, I would encourage every expat partner in a similar situation to do some things differently. Most importantly, prepare yourself well in advance for the amazing giant roller coaster ride you are about to get on, with all its ups and downs. Don't be shy to ask for any support to help you re-establish and continue your life and career abroad, whether from your partner, their company, or experts and associations specialising in expatriate management.

It feels good to realize that I wouldn't have changed any of the major or important decisions. I am truly thankful for the life that I am allowed to live, even though sometimes I have to remind myself of that. For a short, but more than painful episode for everyone involved, I was trapped in a very dark place, so I am also aware that there is not always sunshine. The wealth of experience and personal growth that I have been able to see so far is not taken for granted. Looking at our son and seeing the world together with him, with his eyes, ears and mouth wide open and interested in every little detail, I am just as happy (GLÜCKlich) as I could have ever dreamt of being.

As you can imagine, the next step—repatriating "home" to Austria—will be quite a change and challenge. Brussels, where we are living right now, feels more like home than any of the other destinations we have lived in before. I simply love our apartment, I have given birth to our son here, and he calls Brussels home. I am not looking forward to explaining to him that it will no longer be like that in a couple of months. But am confident that he will find the feeling of home wherever we are.

Something else has changed over the last couple of years: I am proud to be an expat mompreneur, to have built a small, but exciting portable career which I can take along and continue with wherever we go. And last but not least, together with a friend I have founded the association VIE LESA, in Vienna, and throughout Austria, which helps expat partners to re-build their life and career there.

So in any case, repatriation will continue to be influenced by my expat journey—and the roller coaster ride will continue.

14

FROM PIGS TO PINOT - SHANNON DAY

We've decided to do a wine tour in Niagara-on-the-Lake, and I'm about to get on a bike for the first time in years.

Memories of being on a bicycle in China come to mind.

Our friends have their hearts set on cycling from winery to winery so, with a hint of reluctance, we've agreed to it. Like a child first learning to ride, I wobble and sway and then, with an unstoppable smile and a genuine concern for my own safety... I'm off!

Off like the wind, not off in a ditch.

The sun is shining and I'm feeling wild and free because I don't have to worry about the kids. They're happy at home, doing crafts, and having fun with my parents. And also because riding a bike feels foreign and refreshing, and so does the peacefulness of the nature around us.

Our laughter fills the air. To the wineries, we'll go...

Jiangmen City, China (2002)

Employed by a Canadian school board, I spend my days teaching English and drama to Chinese teenagers. There are others like me, but not too many of us. Jiangmen isn't really a destination for tourists, nor would most twentysomethings line up to live here.

There aren't really any nightclubs or nice restaurants to go to. There certainly isn't much of a dating scene, unless you're content sharing a bike with your date and a cage of live chickens. Hardly anyone speaks English and most attempts at speaking Mandarin are met with confused faces that can't even begin to comprehend what you're trying to say.

Foreigners stand out in Jiangmen City. People gawk, overtly. Children point and traffic slows in our presence.

But, other than the stir that's caused while out and about, life there is pretty simple.

One afternoon, I decide to walk from the school over to a nearby village to buy some bananas and have a look around.

The last time I'd ventured home from the village, I'd come across a slavering, wild pig. He'd blocked the dirt path, not with any evil intent but with his enormous, filthy body. I'd been startled at the time and for a brief moment, I'd envisioned him eating me with his giant teeth. He'd sauntered off, instead.

On this humid afternoon, bananas in hand, I don't come across any dirty pigs, but I am confronted by two sweaty men. They stand there, in my way, and their intentions are unclear.

They stare. I force an uncertain grin.

And then, without warning, a woman on a bike rolls up, as if she's sensed my unspoken need to get the hell out of here. She looks about my age, hair pulled back in a messy ponytail.

Her knowing eyes meet mine and, in an instant, she moves forward, off her seat, and I hop on. Bananas in one hand, I grip the seat tightly with the other. We wobble and sway and then, with an unstoppable smile and little concern for my own safety, we're off!

Over potholes and bumps, she pedals. The air is heavy and she's struggling but this woman is determined to take me home.

Our laughter fills the air.

We arrive at the gates of the school, a dominant structure amidst the smog. Neither of us can understand the other's words but we speak anyway, knowing what's being said.

The wine is going to our heads now as we ride back to the B & B. It's been a full day. We're still smiling, though our legs are burning.

We'll get changed and meet our friends at a farm-to-table restaurant. I don't think I'll order the pork tonight.

I am feeling grateful for the freedom of today, though. Even knowing that the more wine I sip, the more likely tomorrow will be an all-day sunglasses day.

But hey, everyone deserves to feel wild and free every once in a while. For the memories that have been stirred, and made, it'll be worth it.

15

BLINDFOLDED AND BACKWARDS - MARCEY HESCHEL

I swore I wouldn't miss that place at all. My pregnancy sickness and food aversions were so intense that if I even saw a person eating noodles or heard the words *mi goreng*, I would start retching like I'd smelled a corpse, or perhaps a reeking durian fruit. I was so unequivocally done with the street food hawkers and their raw hanging chickens that the news of our relocation to Canada came like a Gravol to my nausea.

If I heard one more "no have *lah*" from a store vendor clearly carrying my requested item, I was going to spontaneously combust. "Can you look?" I would say, and magically whatever was "No have *lah*" two minutes before would appear. A simple "don't want to look" would at least have garnered a straight up *c'est la vie*. Eye roll after eye roll had become my modus operandi in dealing with all things Malaysian. The dinner-time mosquito fogging that left its ghostly remnants on our forks and the insanity of the driving style with horn use replacing signal lights had all become noxiously foul.

I vowed to never again climb the 272 steps up to the Batu Cave Temple, because the monkeys were rabid and bound to attack, and the birds sent too many startled tourists away with "good luck". The smog and haze that replaced much of the sunshine created a chill that made our skyscraping infinity pool too cold to enter. Our two-year-old daughter took her toddler swimming lessons in the hot tub instead. She had been on 75 flights before the age of three and had seen more countries than most do in a lifetime.

It was certainly enough. We were impatiently ready to bid adieu to our expatriate comrades and have our belongings packed up in our 3000-square-foot luxury condo, complete with 5 bathrooms. We were certain that we knew what freshness awaited us in the smog-free Rocky Mountain air. What we didn't know was just how much we would actually miss the place we swore we wouldn't miss at all: dear, sweet Malaysia.

That's the thing about taking something for granted. You often don't get a re-do. Once the ignorance wears off, all you are left with is regret and "shoulds". "We should have appreciated that more," or, " We shouldn't have been so eager to leave." Perhaps the silver lining comes in the form of an opportunity to reframe the memories. And doing so is often easiest when I'm walking to my frozen car on a Canadian winter day and thoughts of Langkawi or the Perhentian Islands pop into my mind. I would now eat every noodle in Malaysia to be back on one of her beautiful beaches. Exotic and adventurous was the lifestyle we had been living overseas and it was difficult adjusting back into a more mundane and humdrum grind.

So, as I reflect upon the things I so thought I would never miss about Malaysia, I now see how they changed me and were actually part of a unique and incredible culture that we had the opportunity to experience. There is a negative correlation between ignorance and gratitude. I now understand that more clearly than ever.

Comfort Zones

How truly incredible street food is! For about 5 Malaysian ringgit or $1.50, you can have your absolute fill of Indian or Chinese dishes all made right there by local cooks in a street shop. At the time I found it slightly grotesque and worried intensely about the hygiene, while my colleagues filled their bellies and were no worse for wear. I chose to spend five times as much most days on a pre-packaged basic sandwich from a grocery store frequented by other less adventurous expatriates. This "safer" choice may have kept me from experiencing all sorts of local Malay cuisine. If ever blessed to return I will eat that *hawker laksa* and *mi goreng* all day long, and I will appreciate those bucket-washed raw hanging chickens that make it possible. They are, after all, washed.

Just an Apple

The round and spiky durian fruit might resemble a triceratops egg. The fear of being eaten alive by its pervasive odor of raw sewage is so intense that many condo complexes in Malaysia actually forbid it from entering or being consumed on the premises. Each day, as I would go on my long runs around Mont Kiara and Sri Hartamas, I would pass by jackfruit and durian stands. Retching as I ran, I would reminisce about the fresh raspberries and saskatoon berries of Canadian summers.

Had I opened my eyes with mindfulness at the time, I may have more greatly appreciated the kaleidoscope of mangoes that were available for less than 1 Malaysian ringgit, or about 32 Canadian cents. I may have been mesmerized by our daughter feasting on rambutan, starfruit, and mangosteen. I may have focused more intensely on the taste of pineapple selected from a stand in the afternoon, that likely had been harvested that morning. I stare now at my lacklustre but familiar winter fruit bowl, filled with imported apples, oranges and a pear. Longing for the vibrant and polychromatic varieties available to us in Malaysia, I realize now that I mindlessly focused only upon the repugnance of one incredibly interesting fruit.

Sacred Storytelling

I had the honor of bringing some special visitors to climb the 272 steps of Batu Caves and experience the mysticism of the 400-million-year-old limestone. At the base, the statue of Murugan is a sight to behold. It is 140 feet tall and not only the largest statue of a Hindu deity in Malaysia, but the largest statue in Malaysia. It required 300 litres of gold paint, and early each year Hindus from all over the world pilgrimage here to celebrate the festival of Thaipusam.

It was during this festival that my husband, daughter, and

I first visited Batu. We experienced Batu in its greatest form, as believers displayed their sacrifices while climbing the steps to the top. I remember well the flower garlands and milk we purchased as offerings to Murugan, as well as the overwhelming smell of jasmine incense that permeated the temples. Sticks were placed by the hundreds and the ash that remained was often wiped upon the forehead to purify the soul. We witnessed devotees who not only fasted for weeks before Thaipusam but then pierced themselves with hooks to evoke forgiveness or prayers from the deity. After blessings from a Hindu priest and ash-marked foreheads, we returned to our condo unaware of the cultural magnitude of our experience.

Months later I brought my 70-year-old parents to the top of those stairs and created more incredible memories as we survived the primates. During Thaipusam they ensure the long-tailed macaque monkeys are absent, but the reality of Batu on most other days of the year is that these tyrants unceremoniously dominate a kingdom there. My father had his flower offering pulled from his neck as a monkey jumped on him, hoping for lunch. He threw the flower garland to the ground as we all stood horrified in disbelief. These pilfering sneak-thieves are cute from afar, but far from cute. They have learned that humans have sustenance they desire, and aggressively pursue it. They snatch sunglasses Fagin-style and are more than happy to finish your child's orange Fanta that was in his little hand but a moment ago. Far too many unaware tourists enjoy feeding the monkeys. Amusing to me is a sign right at the base of the 272-stair climb that reads "No exercise". Although I would have loved to run up the stairs for a sacred temple cardio blast, I am quite certain that most visitors find the sign a bit of an oxymoron.

Memories such as these, which make me laugh today, replace the apathy that familiarity had brought. I've reframed the notion that Batu is an overrun tourist attraction guarded by vengeful monkeys, with a much more grateful appreciation for the history, the culture and the experiences I had there with my loved ones. These are the memories great stories are made of.

Incomparable Views

When you're living in such close proximity to the ocean, flights to some of the most exotic beaches on the planet are a dime a dozen. We often took long weekend excursions to places such as Bali, Lombok, the Gili Islands, Langkawi, Sabah, Borneo, and even the Maldives. I would now happily sit for days in the heavy rush hour honking traffic of Kuala Lumpur for a chance to fly to Sri Lanka, then Malé, and await a private Twin Otter flight to a private island resort and overwater villa. I shake my head as I remember how distressed we were that night because our late departing flight was cancelled due to weather, and we had to wait until the next morning to catch another. Distressed! I would gladly experience some of that distress as I write this, on a bitterly cold Canadian January day.

Longing to return to the dream, I recently searched for flights from Calgary to Malé. They begin at over $2000 per person. We paid 10 percent of that from Kuala Lumpur. I doubt a day will ever go by that I do not remember the sight of the Maldivian Islands out the windows of the plane; the colour of electrifying blue that occasionally accompanies a hue of the purest green, and when it is seen, a rare incomparable view.

Had we flown that night, I would never have seen from above the sun shine down upon those islands, for we would have flown in darkness. I now hold gratitude for that delay as it let me see the light.

Filling Buckets

Somehow, diving in a dry suit in the cold Canadian waters doesn't have quite the appeal of being welcomed by the tropical 78-degree underwater world of Southeast Asia. Holding the Advanced PADI diving license I achieved in my younger backpacking days, I was able to experience yet again the breathtaking reefs of Thailand, Indonesia, and Borneo. Most memorable was the day my 73-year-old father agreed to attempt scuba diving for the first time in his life while joining us in Thailand. We rented scooters and made like bandits through the winding roads of the island to the dive resort. The man who once was a precise and skillful dental surgeon, and weekend twin engine pilot, was a proven quick study, and the very next day there we were on a dive boat headed out towards Ko Phi Phi. It just so happened to be the exact place I first learned to dive.

I remember the dive as being one of the greatest of my life. Clouds of tropical fish surrounded us, multitudes greater than I had ever witnessed before. The stunning anemone on these reefs is a fluorescent purple that is striking against the orange clownfish that swim in and out of it, protected from its sting. I compare diving to Buddhist meditation because if anything can help you live in the moment, this is it. The steady focus on your breath, and the awareness of everything around you, bring you solely into the present moment. The colours are so mesmerizing and all senses are on overdrive to an extent that you rarely get caught up in meaningless thoughts. There is a silence that bonds divers after surfacing that only we can understand. It's as if speaking would be disrespectful to the world below you. As you remove your regulator and breathe surface air again, you feel full of gratitude for the experience of a world we were never meant to enter.

I will never forget sharing that truly mindful experience with my father. What I didn't appreciate enough at the time was that living away was not only allowing me to make memories, but was also allowing my loved ones to have a few bucket list adventures of their own.

Rose-Coloured Glasses

Then there was the day on a Thai island when my mother crashed her scooter. Straight ahead of me, on the winding island road, she veered to the left, hit a water ditch, and down she went. I responded as though expletives were my primary vernacular. She popped up from the side of the road, near a palm-covered family dwelling, and shouted something that made everything fall into place. I left her in the care of a local family as I retraced our journey, until I found the spot: the site of the crash she'd *already* had that day, where, under a victimized tree, I found her glasses. As I returned them to her, all I remember was my mother sitting there in pain, but as strong as an ox with her toe bare to the bone. She was shaking her head and blaming the bikes. I happened to see it differently, and perhaps with glasses in place she might have also!

After the news made it back to our villa, my father apprehensively made his way to the rental shop to pay for "those damn bikes." Somehow, absurdly, we walked away paying only $100 in damages for all three casualties. Thankfully they were only bikes. Today, although I wish that I had encouraged a scooter lesson prior to the joyride, I'm amused by this memory that will live forever in my rear view. Sometimes you do not recognize how epic even your calamities can be until the shock wears off and the story are laughed about for years to come.

The Comrades

Often it's who you're with, rather than an experience itself, that makes something enjoyable. Expatriate life for us was full of the "who". When people from all over the world are brought together at the same time to live in the same foreign city for an unknown period, you share a bond of random serendipitous fellowship. The only certainty is that it will end and people will move on. In fact people come and go continuously, and expatriate life is a process of constant greetings and departures. We often develop friendships at farewell parties. We seek only to enjoy the time we have in the present because it's fleeting, and the culture of goodbye is unique.

I would now run all 272 steps up to the temple of Batu Caves blindfolded and backwards, to be back in the company of our dear expatriate comrades. From embassy balls to Sunday afternoon pool days and "Come Dine With Me" dinner parties, it was all a dream, and I spent far too much time complaining about how cold the pool was.

In the Rear View

If hindsight is 20/20, the epiphany is this: we must enjoy where we are in the present moment, because in time this too will change, and leave only memories. I must now appreciate our Canadian home and the proximity to our loved ones, the experience of giving birth to a baby boy in our home country, raising a family with familiar traditions, watching our daughter start kindergarten in a place we know well, and our picturesque Canadian Christmas season that the world dreams of, complete with snow and ice-capped mountains. I may dream of Langkawi or the Maldives on the coldest of days, but there is truly something beautiful wherever we are. We just need to remember to look for it.

16

HOMEMADE HAPPINESS - ERICA LEWANDOWSKI

It was the four of us. We were a young family, living in Florida: a banker, an engineer, and two small kids both under the age of five. My husband and I traveled occasionally, but just for work...and never together. We had lived in Florida for the last ten years and built a comfortable life. We had family close by and good jobs. Our weeks revolved around work schedules and who could pick up the kids from day care before 6pm. Our weekends involved the standard chores of mowing the lawn and grocery shopping, while trying to squeeze in something fun to do with the kids. When the opportunity to move to southern France presented itself, my husband and I jumped on it. We soon found ourselves on our first plane ride together after ten years of marriage, to go to Miami to apply for our visas to move overseas.

Moving to southern France was a romantic idea for us. For our ten-year wedding anniversary we wanted to go to Paris together. Between work and kids we weren't able to make that happen. Magically, it was only six months later we found out we were moving to France. We didn't have a lot of notice or time to prepare. No one in our family knew a word of French. Our family was moving to the land of cheese and wine, croissants and baguettes. It was our first family move, and it was a big one.

I happily started Googling the region, its real estate, and the perfect areas of town to move to. The company we were moving with offered a moving package that generously included moving over our belongings and covering our temporary housing. We were also fortunate enough to have a relocation specialist to help us during our home search. Certainly, with the help of a bilingual specialist, we would find a great home and settle right in!

When we arrived in France, we stumbled out of the plane and it felt like we landed on Mars. The landscape, the language, and the jet lag all blurred together. When we finally met Karin, our relocation specialist, it was pure relief. She was bilingual and had grown up in the area. What more could we ask for? Our family was ready to find a house and we told her our wish list. We didn't need a fancy house. We just wanted a safe, clean house with at least three bedrooms and a bathroom with a bathtub for the kids.

Karin explained to us that there was a large company headquartered in our area. They were a huge employer and constantly had people moving in and out of town. They had specifications for corporate family housing and had lease agreements with the majority of property owners in town. This meant for us that most of the houses for rent in this area went to employees of this company. Our options were quickly narrowed down to the few houses in the area that didn't fit their guidelines. Karin said there were five available homes for us to see.

We spent the next day previewing the houses. The first was located in a cornfield, with no visible neighbors. The second was a huge, cold farmhouse that came with several barns and buildings, and a locked, inaccessible third story. This all seemed a little too strange. The third was a dark, small home with unpainted raw wood walls. Two members of our family had an irrational fear of spiders, so this home was immediately crossed off our list. The fourth home was far outside the city. It was a country home with a 30-minute drive to anything close to civilization. The fifth home was a 3000-square-foot, beautifully renovated 250-year-old home in a quaint village, with a pool, five bedrooms, and three bathrooms. The choice was obvious.

Our new home was everything a North American could dream of when they think of moving to France. The home used to be two old, stone farmhouses. The owners renovated the two houses and built a beautiful connecting room. They left the stones in place so the natural beauty of the stones made up the interior walls of the house. Raw beams were displayed overhead and there were three fireplaces in the downstairs area. It was August and all of the windows were open and overlooked an Olympic-length pool in a beautifully landscaped backyard.

With all of its charm, the home was also beautifully quirky. The master bedroom had a bathtub located next to the bed. It also had a toilet directly across from the bed. No walls, no separation. You could literally step out of the tub and into bed. Or, you could lay in bed and look at the toilet.

We hadn't seen many French houses, so we accepted this as just another experience to embrace.

We moved into the home in September and started settling into our new French dream home. We were enjoying the pool, the open windows, and our new French adventure.

Soon it was October and the season started to change. The weather became cooler and we started closing all the windows. We were beginning to realize that the old, quaint rocks didn't do much for insulation. They did, however, provide a great hiding space for an enormous amount of spiders that decided to make our indoors their home during those cool fall months. I asked the proprietor of our home how to deal with these spiders. *Should we spray? Was there a product or something to get the spiders out?* We were told the spiders that stay in the corners were good luck. They ate the flies. If we really were not comfortable sharing our home with these creatures, we were told the only thing you can do is vacuum them. So, I began vacuuming: the walls, the corners, the beautiful beams. All 3000 square feet was vacuumed so regularly it could have been my full-time job. As someone who loves animals to the point that I've been a long-time vegetarian, I made it a point to quietly apologize to each spider I vacuumed. It's not in my nature to harm anything, so this daily extermination process didn't settle well with me.

One day, we found a large, meaty, hairy spider who had made a web downstairs in a corner by a window. It was too big to vacuum. We didn't know what to do, so we just decided to leave it there. My family decided if "Fangtasia" ever moved from her small corner we would have to figure out a way to get rid of her. Until then, we would watch her.

We watched Fangtasia for almost a year. She became a pet. She built an intricate cyclone web and would catch flies and carry them down into the funnel. Instead of vacuuming spiders, we started catching flies for her and fed her throughout the day. That was the end of my spider vacuuming, and no one in my family is scared of spiders anymore.

As the fall turned into winter, we quickly realized that outside of Florida, fireplaces are used for much more than ambiance. Our house had small space heaters in the upstairs bedrooms, and another in the back corner of the kitchen. There were no radiators and no central heating. In this enormous house, fireplaces were the main sources of heat. Building a fire is a learned skill and as a Floridian, a skill I hadn't mastered yet. My husband would wake up at 4am every day before work and start three fires. It was my job to try and keep them going all day. I have a picture of my children, dressed in pajamas, with their robes on, ski jackets over their robes, scarves and earmuffs on, eating cereal at the kitchen table. They were happy to get out of the house and go to school to keep warm, and I spent the cold mornings in warm cafes studying my French. I would have done just about anything to get out of that freezing house.

We lived mostly out of just one of the two sides of the house. The other was used for storage, a playroom, and a guest bedroom. There were no closets in any of the rooms, but we had a designated changing room that was located on the far side of the house. All of our clothes were kept in this one room, down the hallway from a bathroom. We would shower, then go into the changing room to get dressed. There was no fireplace near the changing room or the bathroom. In the winter months, it was so cold in the changing room you could literally see your breath. Mid-winter of the second year we lived in the house, we ended up making a barrier to close the entrance to the far side of the house. We decided the trouble of trying to keep that half of the house warm wasn't worth keeping the space easily accessible to us. So, mid-winter our house size was effectively cut down to approximately 1300 square feet. We stayed slightly warmer that year. Our beautifully spacious French dream home was starting to become less dreamy.

During those wintry months we used a small heater in the back corner of our kitchen. I would turn this on as soon as I wandered downstairs in the morning to start my coffee or breakfast for the kids. Usually our morning routine would also have me turn on the oven, the microwave, the coffee machine, the dishwasher, or some combination of these appliances. At least once a morning, and quite often more than once, while the heater was trying to run, the circuit would short and we would lose all power to that side of the house. This was extra irritating, because the switch to turn the power back on was at the end of my driveway in the street. Any given morning in the winter, you could have driven by my house and found me mumbling and grumbling some possibly inappropriate words in my pajamas, trying to turn the electricity back on. It was just pure bad luck that the winter season in this area is also the rainy season. My old neighbors probably drank their coffee every morning waiting for the crazy American lady across the street to run outside to the end of her driveway in her pajamas in the rain and yell curse words in English.

We got used to the bathtub next to our bed. It was the only bathtub in the house and having two little kids, it got a lot of use. Our bedroom was directly above the kitchen, and there was a small bathroom right at the entrance of our kitchen. One day we came home from an evening out and immediately stepped in water. There was water flooding our foyer, dining room, kitchen and bathroom. We had no idea where it came from. We cleaned it up and searched for the problem but didn't find anything that would cause such a mess. This happened another two times before we realized what was happening. Every time anyone took a bath upstairs, the water would flow down through the pipes. There was a clog somewhere in a drain, so all of the bathwater would come up through the toilet next to the kitchen. My husband and I spent every evening for four months snaking that toilet, trying to clear the drain. It became a part-time job for both of us each evening. So romantic.

The standard lease in France was a three-year lease, so we made the best of things. We got used to living in the smaller space, bundling up in our ski jackets for breakfast, and keeping the fires going for at least long enough to get the kids to school. We considered the spiders in the corners good luck, and I considered it an opportunity to practice my French cursing skills when it was time to turn the electricity back on in the cold rain. When the owner of the home approached us and told us she would like to sell the house, we tried to contain our grins and began to think about the next place we would continue our adventure.

This time we had lots of French friends to help us through the process of finding a new home. We knew the neighborhood we wanted to move into, but the requirements for the house generally stayed the same. We wanted a safe, clean house with at least three bedrooms and a bathroom with a bathtub for the kids. After two months of looking online and calling on every home that became available in the area, we found a home in the neighborhood we were hoping for. It was a rare find, located directly in front of a school, and with a park in the front yard and another park behind the house. It was walking distance to the square in the village and I had friends who lived in the neighborhood with kids the same age as ours. We made an appointment to see the home immediately. We were the first people to see it, and there were six other people coming that day. We were told that if we liked the house, we had to tell them immediately or it would be gone.

When we walked in, it was small. Much smaller than the previous house. It had just one toilet, in a room smaller than half of my standard-size closet in my home in the States. It was yellow...everywhere. Very, very yellow. I wasn't sure our American king-size bed would fit in the master bedroom.

Then we noticed the radiators in every room, and the warmth. We met the family of four who had lived in the home and raised their family there for the last fifteen years. This house wasn't the home we might have dreamed of when we were living in North America, but something had changed. We had changed. The home was perfect for us. It was clean and warm. There were no extra jobs that would come with this house. No snaking toilets for months. No need to run to the end of our street to turn on the electricity.

No more cleaning three bathrooms! We immediately told the owners this was the perfect house for us.

We downsized our belongings to fit into this home. We got rid of things we didn't need and never used, and it felt good. It gave us freedom. The house was easy to maintain and allowed us the time to travel and enjoy the adventures that France had to offer.

Now that we are back in the United States, we realize we don't want a huge house again. We don't need extra space for things we don't need, we don't want to spend our free time working on projects at home and upgrading everything. We want a comfortable, clean home where we can enjoy being a family together and plan for all of the new adventures that life has in store for us.

17

AN UNWELCOME VISITOR - NICOLA BEACH

I awoke to frenzied barking. The only other time I had heard our dog bark so was when we had an unwelcome visitor in the garden.

On the previous occasion, the barking was followed by screams from our helper who had gone outside to mop the steps. Running to investigate I fully expected to see her being attacked by a machete-wielding madman on the front lawn. Instead, as my helper peeped nervously from behind the gate, I discovered a large brown hissing Sid scuddering under a plant pot inches from my foot. The front door was wide open and had it not been for our valiant little dog going berserk, I think this uninvited guest was planning to slither right on in and find a nice comfy place to curl up and surprise us later on. Normally, I love surprises.

Two heroic security guards found its hiding place and took it away in a shoe box, quickly punctured with breathing holes and firmly secured shut with a great deal of sticky tape.

In the afternoon, the shoebox was returned a with a lovely note saying, *Brown snake most poisonous snake very dangerous snake.*

I was later told that the initial identification was incorrect, and that it was *only* a harmless brown house snake. Well, rather not in my house thank you and no, I didn't need the shoebox back. Also, as a sidenote, snakes are venomous, not poisonous. Bites and stings (for example, from snakes, spiders, or scorpions) are venomous. Eating or drinking something toxic that will make you very sick (like mushrooms, rotten meat, puffer fish or golden dart frogs) is what's poisonous.

As the current barking continued, I crept quickly down the stairs in my pyjamas while the rest of the family slumbered on, wondering whether there was another snake in the garden or whether it was, in fact, the Easter Bunny hiding chocolate, for it was Easter Sunday.

Our dog was frantically scratching at the back door and barking for all she was worth. I saw a flicker of movement beyond the frosted glass. Crouching by her side I peeped through the clear glass border around the frosted section and saw a human eye, stretched wide with fear. I was sure it was fear otherwise I would not have felt so bold; after all, South Africa is infamous for gun crime and armed robbery. He was clearly in flight mode which spurred me into fight mode.

"Who are you? I've called security. My dog will eat you." I screamed at him.

The man curled below our outdoor sink unfurled from

his hiding spot and quietly and urgently began to apologise, backing away, his hands outstretched in supplication.

The dog continued her frantic sounds.

The man, hunched and anxious, was pulling on his jacket, indicating the logo and saying, "It's okay, I'm a security guard." The logo was unfamiliar; he was not one of ours.

The dog's ferocious woof belied her slight build and gentle nature. The man outside surely thought we had a hound from hell though. I shouted and hammered my fists on the window at him. He ran away, and for good measure I let the dog out to make certain he retreated back over the wall, then quickly locked the door.

Not sure what had just transpired, I immediately called security. They assured me the man had been apprehended as he left our property and, rightly or wrongly, shared the whole story with me.

It turns out he was a fare dodger. He didn't have the few coins needed to pay the bus fare to get to work. So rather than face the wrath and most likely physical retribution of the taxi bus driver, he fled the bus, hurdled the security boom to our estate and ran pell-mell through the streets, eventually slipping behind our hedge and hopping over the wall to hide, until he was outfoxed by our dog.

The tragedy was that the guy had a job. He was on his way to work to earn money, but still couldn't make ends meet and had thus tried to ride for free, knowing full well he risked a beating or worse if caught. I was told that his fate had been to be handed over to the aggrieved taxi driver. This left me with many uncomfortable thoughts and questions.

What became of the fare dodger? It would have been

easy to assume that he was a lowlife, a gambler or drug addict who had squandered his pay-check. But I wondered, did he have a family? Young children at home waiting for their father to return? Was he short of money because one of his family members got sick and racked up medical bills? Or because his landlord had jacked the rent up? Or because he was scraping together money for school fees, books and uniforms? Where was he now? At home nursing his bruised ego? In a hospital ward, his injuries being nursed? Or in a ditch? All these guilty questions swam through my head on a morning when our own children would soon be happily bouncing out of bed and rushing downstairs to see if the Easter Bunny had visited.

And what of the taxi driver? Those guys have a reputation for being hard-as-nails. They rule the roads; you are taught never to confront a taxi driver no matter how dreadful or dangerous their driving is, as many are armed. I'm sure that just as the fare dodger genuinely couldn't afford the fare, the taxi driver equally could not afford to lose the fare, or encourage fare dodgers by inaction, by being lenient and understanding. Undoubtedly, he too had bills to pay and dependants who were relying on his wages.

And equally, what if we hadn't had a dog? What if the man had remained undetected in our garden and I had let the children out to play? What if I had left the back door open, as I often did in the morning to let fresh air blow through, and he had entered our home via the kitchen, passing the knife block? How desperate was this man and to what lengths would such a desperate man go? These are answers I don't like to dwell upon.

Living somewhere full time, you are drawn beyond the anonymity of the street beggar glimpsed fleetingly from a hotel taxi or the thief who takes something from you in the blink of an eye while you arrive at the airport for your holiday. Instead you become aware of the social and political backdrop driving the poverty, and perpetuating crime wherever you live. You learn the names and faces of those around you, parking attendants, security guards and domestic workers, often living day to day and hand to mouth.

Previously, when living in West Africa, we had a driver. He worked for us for five years, and during that time we learned about his family and his life story. Like so many, life had given him few opportunities and many hurdles. He dreamed of returning to his village and opening a motorcycle repair shop, but city life was tough, his dream always out of reach, pie in the sunny sky.

Despite decent wages, free accommodation and additional assistance from us, there was nothing we could do when he returned from a trip to his village and told us that he had lost a child. Far away in the bush, his eldest child had succumbed to an unknown illness. Possibly due to a bad mosquito bite, the local medicine man had told him. Furthermore, every trip home was a terrible drain on his resources, as extended family would be expecting gifts and financial support. A single wage packet would not just be supporting a nuclear family, but often an entire community.

When we eventually moved away, I was sobbing at the airport and my parting words to him as we said our farewells were, "Look after your family." I didn't mean for him to take my words literally, and abscond with the company car, sell it and disappear with the proceeds, but that's how he interpreted it. With a new boss arriving in country, he had no job security; new brooms often sweep clean, replacing staff with somebody of their own choosing.

And when you see daily how desperate lives are, rather than anger or confusion you are more likely to feel compassion and understanding, and even a dollop of admiration for such an audacious crime. What would you have done in his shoes? Quite possibly exactly the same thing.

There are four truths to take away from this story, four more lessons that I have learned on this expat journey. Firstly, if you live in Africa, a dog is an effective snake and burglar deterrent. Secondly, snakes are venomous, not poisonous, unless you decide to eat one and it disagrees with you. So, don't go eating wild snake willy-nilly. Thirdly, my husband can sleep through anything: epic thunderstorms, crying newborns in the night, and our dog sounding an almighty intruder alert.

Lastly and most profoundly, we all do the best we can for our family. As expats that's exactly what we do every time we move, we try to give our family the best financial and cultural advantages and the biggest adventures. But sometimes the actions we take to ensure our family's wellbeing can involve a morally questionable decision, whether it's handing a scared man over to security and onward to the mercy of an angry taxi driver to ensure your loved ones are safe, whether it is beating the living daylights out of a fare dodger to protect your livelihood, or whether it is stealing a car to improve your lot.

The unwelcome visitor made me consider this truth. An uncomfortable truth that hides on the dark side of our gilded expat bubble.

18

FINDING FULFILLMENT ON THE MOVE - GABRIELA O'MALLEY

A year into what was my eighth relocation, with both of my girls in school full-time, and feeling fairly settled, my mind was still spinning. We drove cross-country and were downsizing our life from a big New England-style home to a small cozy apartment surrounded by gigantic redwood trees. I watched exciting chapters emerging around me. I saw everyone so happy and busy, getting ready to kick off their new beginnings. My husband started a new job, my children buzzed with the new school, new activities, and friends. It seemed there was lots going on in their lives. They all left each morning. I felt all I had were the unending to-dos I had been doing for years. This time, home alone, I had nothing exciting going on in my personal chapter.

The reality hit me harder than my 40s. I started blaming myself for having missed so many opportunities to invest more in my personal growth. Battling and arguing with my strong, opinionated inner critic, I had never felt more lost and confused in my entire life. I felt I had fallen in the shadows of unlived potential and I didn't like it. I was craving a greater sense of personal fulfillment and enriching progress. People talked about going back into the workforce and meeting with recruiters, as if they had been protecting my treasure all these years. I started looking for answers on the outside, hoping people would tell me where to look or give me straight one-sentence answers. I was asked so many times what my unique value proposition was. I discovered that running was my space to burn the frustration of not having an answer for it.

I'd spend the next six years running, and investing in myself. Over a thousand miles later, diving into the deepest corners of myself, and gaining fresh academic knowledge and training, I finally found my answers.

Serial Reinvention

Every time I've uprooted my life, it feels as if a series of dimensions are created. In the snap of a finger, I'm living between the past and the present, at the same level of intensity. That has always been at the center of all my transitions: the past gradually shrinks, while the present starts growing fast. The role I held depended on where I was on the wheel of life. I closed chapters and opened new ones, over and over. I was a newlywed in some, a pregnant woman with a full-time job in another, and a mother of a toddler, with a high-risk pregnancy, at another point. And, for many years, I was a mother of two girls who learned to give away toys with each move, while watching how I too would leave pieces of my life to close friends, Goodwill, and even the movers.

Interestingly, I found that, seasoned expat or not, being at the starting line of a new life is daunting. For example, our relocation to Singapore was my first as a mother with a four-month-old girl, and one significantly different from anything I'd been through before. Within weeks of arriving, my husband had gone to India for a whole week. I didn't know a soul in the city and I felt the sinking, lonely feeling of being so far away from everything and everyone. You could say I had some experience, as I had four relocations—abroad and local—behind me. Still, it was intimidating.

Uprooting your life is a big deal. It is crazy, enriching, and complex.

I crossed each dimension with periods of transition and a deluge of to-dos that would support the whole family in settling in a new life. That alone was a full-time job. I've spent so many years mastering the art of saying *adios* and creating new lives. In that cycle of packing one life, followed by interim periods than can last weeks or months, to then create a new one—from scratch—I've learned a lot of tricks and have become an expert in fields never covered in any of my many years of academic education. I didn't know then I was gaining any sort of expertise, but I did. Anyone with a life on the move does.

And how do you explain the emotional roller coaster that goes with it all? That alone deserves an entire book. The highs and lows wrapped with joy, intensity, newness, adventure, and plenty of uncertainty. I've felt supremely overwhelmed and exhausted. At other times I held a high level of stamina I wish I still had today, losing and regaining my mind, sometimes several times a day. This all came with the blessing of not facing health issues, but I know of those who have, or who have encountered bereavement, lost jobs, or divorces.

Those dimensions in my journey brought a perspective on life from which I continue to learn, life lessons that have influenced my understanding of faith, cultures, race and traditions. They showed me the universality of love, friendship, family and grief. And the individual pursuit of happiness and fulfillment we all crave.

Family Strength

In the fifteen years of my nomadic journey, my biggest achievement, I would say, is having my family in one piece. The tests of life-altering experiences forge incredible strength and resilience. I feel a satisfying sense of success when I see my girls interact in the world with kindness and resilience, culturally respectful and openly curious about the diverse world we live in. I've learned to foster endurance. I've understood, in action, the meaning of meticulously protecting my family, and the less-discussed subtle challenge of crafting a safe, loving home literally anywhere: a short-term place, a shoe-sized apartment, or a thousand-square-foot house. Home really *is* where family is.

Going through a myriad of moves while raising children is challenging and exquisite. I make a conscious effort to give my daughters enough credit. They are my greatest teachers. I've watched them adapt to new cultures, blend easily into diverse new environments, and pick up new languages faster than anyone. Without doubt, it expands their curious minds and strengthens their confidence and sense of independence.

In their little uncomplicated world, any travel plans can get confused with a relocation.

On one occasion, we had just arrived from Madrid to Connecticut. After a couple of short-term housing arrangements, we had finally moved into our new home. One morning, my oldest daughter, then six years old, overheard my phone conversation about some plane tickets and hotels. As she was enjoying her Cheerios, she very casually and calmly said, *"Mommy, when are the movers coming to start packing?"* I couldn't understand at first what she meant, until I explained we were planning to fly to Playa del Carmen, in Mexico's Riviera Maya, for the spring break. I felt some guilt and wondered if I was a bad parent, depriving my children of a traditional rooted lifestyle. Then I remembered I grew up having one. There are no right or wrong paths, it's what's happening inside the family that matters.

Seven years later, we had just relocated to our 11th home. My youngest daughter, now 11 years old, made a birthday card for her sister's 13th birthday. She drew the four seasons of the year on the cover, and inside wrote, "Happy Birthday! I know that we are going through a lot but all year round, every year, though seasons change, I love you."

I know that both of my daughters are growing with a culturally open mindset, welcoming change. It will be great to witness how it will continue to impact their lives.

Maintaining Continuity

Learning how to maintain continuity in your life is an art. With a 'life on the move', we have to both switch worlds and catch up with life. This has been my biggest challenge, and one that has impacted my life in ways I didn't foresee.

After the slowdown period from the hectic stress of the move, come the demands of settling a new life: setting up new doctors, schools, activities, jobs, and friends; for some, all with children in the equation. It is during this busy time, with our minds occupied by the demands of absorbing the richness of the new environment and adjusting our lifestyle, that we neglect timely actions that are fundamental to our experience of personal fulfillment, success, and a sense of achievement.

Our unique stories are like fingerprints, and here, I speak from my own experience and from what I have witnessed. Timely actions are those specific choices we each make every day that bring us closer to experiencing progress, growth and our personal sense of achievement and contentment. This encompasses the art of learning to bring continuity to our life, and is what moves us closer to living with purpose and realizing our own destiny.

Time doesn't wait for us. It's so easy to get caught up in random, unimpactful, and sometimes superficial stuff that will contribute little to our personal goals. Every choice we make is fundamental to how we experience progress.

Making the Right Choices

Find clarity and protect your self-identity. In the process of relocation, an underlying challenge is losing clarity and self-identity. Not all careers are portable; not all new destinations guarantee a new job. Climbing the ladder of change and transition can include having to learn a new language, navigating a big city, opting—or having—to stay home to raise the family, or arriving after uprooting a well-established life.

We're so distracted by navigating our new lives, wearing many hats, while becoming the unbreakable support system for the family. The first thing we neglect is ourselves. We can get lost and forget who we are, which is easier than you'd imagine. This is why taking timely actions is critical to maintaining continuity in our pursuit of personal fulfillment, success, and a sense of achievement. Losing continuity can lead to lost opportunities.

Secondly, search for self-knowledge. One essential choice for a 'life on the move' apprentice is to cultivate a deep understanding of self: core values, personal resources, potential, abilities, dreams, and goals. The foundation of self-knowledge is an awareness compass in your mobile life with all the demands of change, adaptation, transition, and creation. Assessing self-transformation is pivotal in the ability to thrive. That's where the treasure is.

In our own unique way, we discover and create our own experience, and make our own choices. There are many ways to thrive in the art of having a life on the move. I will leave you with three pieces that could fit in anyone's life puzzle—regardless of age, number of children, career, or place in the world.

Piece number one: *prepare* your mind to help you understand that with uprooting your life, you're saying goodbye to all that was part of that previous life. For the months or years that follow, the past turns to memories, relationships transform, and travel logistics becomes a top transferable skill. Missing your old comfort-zone routines, family, and friends, is very normal, and unavoidable. It should not be taken lightly.

Preparing your mindset will help you let the challenging periods pass and come back, but not stay and take over, holding you hostage with sadness, anger, or resentment.

Piece number two: *plan* to make time to invest in you. If you don't have time for yourself, you don't have a life; hard, but true. Spend time getting to know who you are in your own wheel of life. List your life's preferences and core values. Know what brings you joy and fulfillment. Nourish your strengths, qualities, dreams and goals. Keep this as your personal well of resources for progress and fulfillment, then build a plan and make the decision to keep taking action.

The final piece: *create* steps to crystallize your plan. Write down the options that would match the well of resources you've created and that would fit into your current life to help you reach your goals for the present, and the future. Small or big, it doesn't matter. What matters is to give your goals continuity.

19

THE MOVE - HELENE BENOIT

Moving is my number one drug and I'd say that's arguably true for expats in general. We dream of it, we anticipate it and we dread it. It's saying sayonara to horrid traffic, long winters or humid mosquito-infested nights, the noisy rooster in the next-door yard or even the complicated friendship we don't really know how to deal with. It also means pulling up all those budding roots, saying goodbye to new best friends, your favorite bakery, the view from the kitchen window or the nanny who's been taking care of your kids since day one. So from the day we land in our new location, the next move is lurking in the back of our minds; at least it is for me! Yet, some moves are harder than others.

The year was 2008; we had just rounded off our first year in Luanda, Angola. I had reached cruising altitude. I knew where to go to buy the nice meat and where to get my Brazilian coffee. I knew the doctor's office like my back pocket and knew you had to stock up when your favorite this or that appeared in the store. I'd gone through an unusual number of nannies to find someone I could trust, we'd just moved into the best house I've ever lived in, and we had a nice, big group of friends around us. Of course, there were things that weren't as good. Grocery shopping was a real torment; everything was either horrendously expensive or of dubious quality. The traffic stole my husband's life and energy and made any improvised social event almost impossible. But shining above it all, I'd been offered a job, a real job, as homeroom teacher for grade four at the international school. I'd translated documents, asked for police records in several countries and my work visa was on its way. I was so happy, back in Norway for the summer, doing my visa work... life was good!

Then came the call.

"We're leaving for Siberia." My husband's voice was wobbly over the phone. The rug was pulled from under my feet. My world tumbled. The accusation, "What did you do?" hung silently in the air between us. Something was broken, something important: the trust I had that everything that happened was a jump forward, that my husband was a bright star and that everything would always evolve in a positive direction; the idea that I had some kind of control over my life. The Gulag. We were being sent to the Gulag.

My journey back to pack up the house was heavy. Having Paul's replacement continuously forgetting things in our house, suddenly just standing in my living room every Sunday lunchtime, made it even more apparent that our time in Angola was up and that my husband had been found wanting. The day school started back up, I cried. I wasn't part of the team. I was home but my dream was gone. When I tried to imagine Siberia, my mind painted an image of grey. Grey skies, grey buildings, grey people. I was going behind the Iron Curtain (weird how your childhood imagination lingers). The only silver lining was that I had one good friend there. Anita, my trusted sister-in-arms in Luanda, had been transferred to that exact city just a couple of months before.

We landed in Moscow on a November evening. I quickly felt I'd fallen into a Kafka novel. We walked down interminable empty corridors, being ushered here and there by the odd uniformed person behind empty desks. In the end we found ourselves in front of a big black door, with a glass wall on one side where uniformed people hustled past without giving us a glance. Were we in a parallel universe? I even banged on the glass wall, out of pure frustration. Had we been forgotten? Were we in the right place? The minutes were so long, I could feel my hair turn grey. Suddenly the door burst open and a beautiful blonde woman in a long, shiny, leather coat smiled at us through the drifting snow. "Passengers for Tyumen?"

From a Kafka novel, I was thrust into Harry Potter's magical world. As we boarded the old Tupolev plane we were beckoned left instead of right and found ourselves in a little compartment with dimmed lights. Through a curtain, I could see a man in slippers scratching his bald head as he sat down in a leather chair. There was a picture in a wood frame on the wall in front of him. I was tucked between a Russian babushka, looking like a live version of a matryoshka doll, and a young girl. Paul sat in the row behind with the kids. I was trying to hold it together as all the nerves of the last months in limbo were coming towards the end. Then I saw it. The girl had a pet—a pet snail, no less, and she was feeding it cucumbers. I started crying. In my mind there was no way we would ever get to our next location, the next chapter in our lives, in this weird contraption. But we did.

We arrived safely in Tyumen five hours later, before dawn. In the car to the hotel they played the Russian pop song my crazy Russian friend had made us line dance to a couple of months before in a previous life, in Angola.

When we woke up the next morning, it wasn't in a Gulag, but under a bright blue Siberian sky. We called our friends, who took us out for lunch and introduced us to the beauties of our new home town...and our new future.

20

DATING OUT OF MY LEAGUE - CHANTALLE BOURQUE

Few people asked me "Why?" when I announced my decision to move from Canada to the Middle East to pursue a teaching opportunity in Abu Dhabi. There were few good reasons not to go. Personally and professionally, it was the perfect time for a change. Adventure, travel, and living in a country where the bitter cold air didn't assault my face four, to six, to nine months of every year all added up to a brilliant decision, one that needed no serious contemplation. Teaching and living abroad had always been on my radar. It was simply time to make it happen.

The lack of anxiety regarding my departure was not in any way related to the quality of life, or lack thereof, that I had in Calgary. I had supportive administrators and colleagues that most teachers only dream of having. I had the opportunity to travel frequently, seeing the likes of the Galapagos Islands, Costa Rica, Nicaragua, and Washington DC whilst being a paid chaperone.

Simply put, my excitement in looking forward to this new

adventure was not a result of an unfulfilled life in Calgary. I knew leaving the niche I had made myself in the eight years since I moved there would be difficult, and this mostly because of the people I was leaving behind. My friends who had become family would be impossible to replace. In preparing for the move, I did ask myself: would the UAE offer enough to fill my love bucket in addition to satiating my appetite for adventure and travel?

When discussing my initial feelings about moving overseas with my friend Hailey, I gave it the following analogy. Consider Calgary to be Mr Right: your great love, your safe place, your comfort. But, you're just not ready to settle down yet. So, you take a leap of faith, and leave your loyal friends and family behind...to start DATING BRADLEY COOPER!

Yep. And at first, it is mind-blowing. There are hardly any thoughts of your last relationship, because this new guy is so handsome and worldly and different from all the other ones you've dated. He is totally out of your league, and you are enjoying it as long as you can, because you know it won't last. Abu Dhabi and the UAE were my hall-pass-worthy rebound from a (temporary) break-up with Canada.

In no particular order, here are the best things my new man had to offer.

He was HOT.

"Winter" took on a new meaning in the UAE. It became the three to four weeks where I could shut off my AC, and needed to remember to throw on a sweater if I was going out past dark.

"But won't you miss the seasons changing?" Quite simply, the answer to this is a resounding NO. I relished in not having to mentally and physically prepare myself for the onslaught of frosty air, windshield scraping, and numb extremities that are synonymous with Canadian winters.

This warmer weather also meant being able to use the outdoors as my playground year-round. Running, which used to be an activity limited to the spring and summer for this fair-weather jogger, became something I did three or four mornings a week. Feeling the hot sun on me is something I used to yearn for and escape to. Being able to walk out my front door and quite literally have it right there in my face year-round was an absolute dream.

He was the beachy, surfer type.

There is something about seeing the ocean and living in its proximity that is so peaceful and rejuvenating. There are no shortages of sandy shores and beautiful beaches in and surrounding the UAE. In my two years there, I saw but a fraction of them.

Saadiyat Island was a personal favourite, its turquoise hues a colourful reminder of how fortunate I was to live in such an exquisite part of the world. The freedom of being able to drive my car to spend an afternoon at the beach, no matter the time of year, is something I don't think I could ever tire of.

. . .

He was fun and exciting.

"Bradley" also offered new outings and activities that I couldn't take part in back home. Whether it be in the shape of camel races at the crack of dawn, or in the form of a beach party, dancing with our toes in the sand long past sunset, I found myself enamoured with the slew of new things to see and do.

Popular with the expat community, Friday brunches were an all-day food and drink fest. You could often find me poolside, binging on roast beef and Coronas, eyeing up the seafood station. In fact, some places had so much food on offer your entrance came with a map of the area. Take the second exit to the sushi bar, and the first exit to your right for the dessert table. Essentially a map to my heart.

For those of us who like to diversify our weekly itineraries with activities that are not akin to a luxe frosh week, you could choose anything from a day at the water park or desert camping, to cave swimming or scuba diving. There was no shortage of new activities to try out, which kept things fresh and exciting.

He has cool friends.

The proximity of the UAE to various exotic locales was also something that this new relationship. Road trips to the Rockies were replaced with day trips snorkelling in Oman. Long weekend trips to Lebanon, Singapore, Paris and Prague replaced the North American getaways that I'd been used to. In less than half the time it would take me to fly to my home-town in Canada from Calgary, I could be sitting in a hammock in the Maldives. Living in a city with an airline that was positioning itself as a hub for international travel came with the perk of direct flights that would make any globetrotter drool. Making the most of this became central to my love affair with the Middle East.

With such an impressive array of things to offer, it was hard to be nostalgic about what I'd left behind, especially at first. The novelty of an exotic lifestyle was more than enough to keep any longing for home at bay. It was, after all, what I'd bargained for when I'd made the decision to live abroad. You do it for all the wonderful things, places and people you would have otherwise never encountered. You do so to meet other wanderlusting souls like yours. You do so to see life from a completely different perspective, and to gain a better appreciation of where you come from. You do so, because turning down a date with Bradley Cooper is something no one with a pulse should ever do.

But, after two years of desert living, it was time to think about where this relationship was going. Despite the many attractions, there were some things that my life with Bradley/Abu Dhabi could not provide, hard as he may try. It was time to decide whether or not this new life would work over the long term. Realistically, was I ready to permanently trade in my great life in Canada for one in Abu Dhabi? Would my new life always feel like this: enlivening, different and luxurious? Or, would the novelty soon wear off, leaving me longing for the familiarity, community and family I'd nurtured in Calgary for over a decade? Would a shiny facade soon make way to a colder reality? One that was more transient than permanent, and, at times, more surface than substance?

Before the love affair could go entirely cold, I made the decision to end our relationship and rekindle with Mr Right. I was fortunate that he took me back, no questions asked. He was maybe even proud of me and my adventurous spirit, and happy to welcome me home: a me that was a little better than when I left. A me that took in and cherished all the good that came with living in a strange land, whilst also recognizing the richness of what I had temporarily put on hold. A me that never underestimated what Mr. Right gave me: a niche and community that I immensely cherished and valued, and that would always feel like home.

He also took me back with an understanding that this was likely not the last time I'd leave him in search of new ventures and thrills. Though he holds a majority stake in my heart, he understands that there also exists an undeniably large piece of my being and soul that needs to be on the move. This is the same part of me that needs to explore new places, and the growth that comes with change. This part of me is loud, and only silenced by leaping from my nest. The self-knowledge that comes from this allows for, the learning that is innate in packing up all your belongings to start anew in a foreign land is quite simply too good to pass up.

So, is it possible to have it all? Can I blend the comforts of home with the inebriating attraction of a globetrotting lifestyle? I hope the answer is yes. I hope that I can find the right mix between settling in my home base, and keeping a spirit that is light enough to keep discovering the world around me in a way only living abroad allows me to. I hope to find balance in nurturing the part in me that needs community while also answering to my traveling spirit – the me that relishes in the wonderment and awe of new places, and all the experiences that living in them brings. I truly hope that I can find someone with whom I can share all of this. The person who, like me, will only feel whole when his heart is full with both a sense of home and a sense of adventure. That is when I know I will have found my person. And when I do, even Bradley won't stand a chance.

(Bradley, if you're reading this: just kidding. Call me?)

21

VOYAGE AND A JOYOUS RESIDENCE - MARGO CATTS

"It's not what you know; it's who you know."

Can we rephrase this? (And not just to fuss about "whom".) Yes, the tangles of living abroad can be smoothed out substantially when you know the right people. But my first lesson about tangles taught me that it's what you *don't* know that gets a person in trouble in the first place.

Expat life rides on a current of paperwork, permits, and passports, and in Saudi Arabia the essential one is known as an *iqama*. This gem of an ID card shows you're allowed to be there (not a given in a country that closely controls visitors), conduct business, rent a home, have a car, and enter and exit the country freely.

They don't just hand these things out like smiley stickers. To even get the process started you need a citizen sponsor (for most expats that's an employer). Then you have to go through a series of medical tests roughly equivalent, both in breadth and invasiveness, to what livestock might go through before being shipped across a border. And then do it again after you've arrived because...just do it, okay? At the border itself you're fingerprinted and photographed, and when all of it—sponsor, photo, fingerprint, a substantial sum of money, and probably a digestive inventory of your most recent meal—is assembled into a file peppered with the proper stamps, that little buff card appears.

But...that would take time. Dear Husband had already been there four months when I was due to arrive, and wanted us to start our new life with a "Cheers to the next adventure" reunion holiday. How could we if I was confined to Saudi Arabia for some time after I arrived? As any Saudi getting on a weekend flight to Dubai will tell you, Saudi Arabia is not a holiday kind of place.

"How about this?" Dear Husband suggested by phone one morning, after he—nine time zones away—had been stewing on the problem all day. "You fly to Doha, in Qatar, and I drive to meet you. We spend the weekend there and drive back together. It's only six hours from Riyadh. I don't have to take any vacation days, no extra flights, and fuel is almost free around here."

It worked. We were pampered in a lovely hotel and enjoyed the sights. I de-jetlagged, and at the end of the weekend we loaded up the car and headed for the border.

After clearing the Qatari side of the border, we wound through barricades and razor wire to the Saudi side. There, it quickly became clear that the man in the lone booth was not accustomed to seeing non-residents enter the country for the first time. He puzzled over my passport. He asked what was in the bins stacked in the back seat, squinted at how big they were, how they were wedged in place, and then took my word for it that they held only clothes and household items. He disappeared into the guardhouse, came back out, disappeared again. Finally, he stamped the passport, pasted something in it, wrote something in Arabic, and handed it back. Nailed to a post was a sign with the only English I could see, which wished me, "Voyage and a joyous residence." I took it as a blessing and crossed into the Kingdom of Saudi Arabia with a sigh of relief.

Next order of business: *iqama*. I had arrived a couple of months before a weeklong national holiday, and Dear Husband, feeling confident, had already booked an actual, leave-the-country vacation. Surely that was plenty of time to get my *iqama* in place. In the words of basically everybody who barely understands what you're asking, "No problem, no problem."

For a nation that's absolute about a lot of things, Saudi Arabia is also a country with a rather fuzzy relationship with procedure, so what's required from whom, on what day, in what place, with which stamps and signatures and level of argument, tends to vary. A lot. Most companies therefore employ Saudis, used to navigating those shifting sands, to handle visa matters. The job of my personal facilitator, given that a spouse visa is a lower priority than an employee's, fell somewhere down the power rankings to a man I'll call Faisal, a freelance fixer available at an appropriate price.

Within a couple of weeks I was able to give him the locally verified medical report (re)asserting my good health, my payment, and my passport. Days ticked by. Weeks ticked by. "No problem, no problem," was the answer, whenever Dear Husband asked Faisal what was going on. "Next week, insha'allah." Our departure date on an Indonesian trip that was already booked and paid for drew closer. And closer.

Finally we figured out why nothing was happening: the lone border guard in that frontier outpost had not taken my picture or fingerprint; whether by ineptitude or lack of equipment, it didn't matter. My file was incomplete. However, Faisal said there was an office that could do it at a (relatively) nearby mall. Finally! Thank you!

Except...the office was closed. At least, the office for women was. There was an office for men elsewhere in the mall, but I lacked the proper chromosomes to use it. I was a woman, you see, and therefore could not have my picture and fingerprint taken in an office that men frequented and where men worked, using machinery meant for men. There was a paper taped to the door of the women's office with something handwritten in Arabic, and signage around the door in Arabic, but, at a visa-and-passport-related office, nothing for foreigners to read. Naturally. When we tried to ask a mall security guard about the office, the gist seemed to be that, well, it's open when it's open. Hit-or-miss is a problem because you're not allowed to drive? Huh. Anyway, good luck with that!

With international departure looming, hit-or-miss wouldn't work even if I could have driven myself there. The only solution was to go, in person, to the actual mother ship passport office in the heart of the government zone of Riyadh. Reluctantly, Faisal agreed to meet us there and walk our embarrassing American selves from office to office until we could get my problem solved. Dear Husband's secretary, Hassan, a Somali man who'd lived in Saudi Arabia for nearly thirty years and spoke far better English than Faisal, wisely decreed that we would not survive this outing without him and joined us.

"Entrance," said a sign in English, at the door of the ministry for visas and passports. It was the last English I saw. I tagged along, blindly, wherever Faisal led. Can you help us in this office? No, upstairs. This one? No, more upstairs. Maybe around the corner. Here? No, downstairs, for sure. The request for someone to just take my picture and fingerprint seemed utterly baffling to everyone we met.

Finally someone said, with some degree of confidence, that the place for *women* to get a fingerprint and picture was through a separate entrance around the back of the building. And really, that should have been our starting assumption. The catch? All the men facilitating my adventure would have to wait outside while I went in alone, speaking no Arabic, unable to read a single character on the signage, in an effort to accomplish business that none of the Arabic speakers around me had been able to puzzle out to this point.

I tried, I swear. I stepped into that door like Jonah saying, "Look! A whale! I wonder what's inside!" I entered a vestibule with blacked-out windows, then after the door clamped shut behind me, passed into a room with desks, and clerks, and lots and lots and lots of black-clad women pressing toward them. I threaded between women, most of whom looked at me but glanced away as soon as I made eye contact. "English?" I tried a few times, feebly, but no one volunteered. All the clerks were busy at their stations, and there was no freaking way I was going to shove myself in front of women who were already suffering as much as I was, thank you very much, and didn't need some foreigner demanding service ahead of them. There was also no freaking way I was going to take a spot at the end of some random line without knowing what it was for. I went back outside.

Faisal, the facilitator, shrugged. Hassan, the secretary, stuck his hand out. "Give me your phone," he said. I did, and he entered his number and handed it back. "Go inside and give this to somebody. I will tell her what you need."

Back into the whale I went. This time I saw a clerk who appeared to be supervising rather than helping customers, and shoved the phone in front of her. After a brisk conversation she returned the phone and held out her hand.

"Passport," she said. I obeyed, and she pointed me to one door as she disappeared through another. I stepped into the back of a windowless room jammed with women, black fabric against black fabric, arms raised, papers and passports waving, and just one station at a distant counter occupied. But at each workstation—hallelujah!—was a camera and a fingerprint reader.

The woman holding my passport appeared behind the counter and sat at a second workstation. The volume rose and the crowd pressed tighter. The woman tapped at the computer for some moments without looking up, then held up my passport, snapping it a bit to beckon me forward. Was it possible? Would she actually take my picture? And would it be a picture of my beaten face after I shoved myself in front of all these women who might have been trying to get attention for hours?

I reached and pushed, but I didn't have to go far. The

woman stood and stretched toward me with the passport. "No match," she yelled over the women's heads.

"What?"

"No match," she repeated, shaking her head firmly.

I fumbled for my phone, dialed Hassan again, and got the phone into the woman's hand before she escaped. Another quick, clipped conversation, and she handed the phone back to me. "Come outside," Hassan said. "I will explain."

No, no, no, no, *no*. Not outside. I didn't just come *this* close to a female camera and female fingerprint reader with a female operator in a female office to bail out now. But the woman had turned away and the crowd had closed. There was nowhere else for me to go. I went out the way I came, and the whale spit me out on the frying-pan concrete.

Faisal took my passport and pointed to the Arabic handwritten on the page that noted my entry into the country.

"No match," he repeated. "Your immigration record has a different number. It is a mistake."

I didn't know the appropriate Arabic curses for that situation, but I did know my own. The exemplary public servant I had encountered at the border, the man deployed to the utmost and dullest outpost of the frontier, given one thing to do—enter my information and copy the assigned entry number onto my passport page—had written down the wrong number. A sloppy pen stroke. A mental slip. No match. No picture for you.

"Can't she fix it, inside? It's hand written. She had a pen. She could just change it."

"No," Faisal said. "To change needs a stamp."

"And she doesn't have a stamp."

"No."

Naturally.

"You go now," Faisal went on. "I will finish. No problem, no problem. You can do nothing. Nothing to do. I will finish."

He started leading us toward the main ministry entrance (also, coincidentally, the direction of our car), repeating the phrases in varying order. Suddenly I realized an older, heavier man walking toward us had thrown his arms wide. "Mr. Steve!" he called to Dear Husband in a booming voice. "Habibi!"

Hassan greeted him, as did Faisal. Even though I couldn't understand the Arabic, the body language was perfectly clear: in the passage of an instant, Faisal had been displaced as the Man In Charge and he was now seething with underclass resentment.

"This is Walid," Dear Husband said. Walid was another freelance fixer and visa facilitator. And, I quickly ascertained, a more expensive and important one. He asked Dear Husband why we were there, and his brow furrowed as he learned that we were having...*problems*.

He turned on Faisal. He interrogated. Faisal answered. Walid turned back to Dear Husband to ask more questions in English. Why had this job been entrusted to anyone but him to begin with? He, after all, had just had the Crown Prince in his home. He was very important, and could make things happen with the snap of his fingers. Back to Faisal. More interrogation. More argument. Lots of posturing and gesturing, white-robed columns leaning forward and leaning back. I couldn't understand a word, but language was unnecessary. My passport had become a piece of meat, with the alpha male combatants snapping and growling and circling around it.

Our group set off toward the main entrance. Jonah and the whale behind us, now we were on our way to Oz with its Wizard, a hidden, mythic figure that held both a pen *and* a stamp, as well as a willingness to implement them in the service of a female. I was Dorothy, Dear Husband the all-heart Tin Man, Hassan the multi-lingual brain of the Scare-crow, while two Cowardly Lions snarled at each other to claim the role of the group's sole protector.

In we went, past the Entrance sign, Walid and Faisal talking over each other to a man in a small office. Passport, yes. Papers, yes. Typing. Then two English words floated out of the patter of competing Arabic: *system down*. The man at the desk put his palms up. *System down.*

Really? This was it? *This* was how everything was going to end? With a network failure we might have been ahead of hours or weeks ago if *someone* (ahem, Faisal, Mr. No-prob-lem-no-problem-insha'allah-tomorrow-can't-be-bothered...) had noticed the number problem himself?

We went back out into the sunshine just as the midday call to prayer sounded and offices began to close. For once, Walid and Faisal were in agreement: we should go home. Walid would call us later. He would make the photo office at the mall open for us after the next prayers at the end of the afternoon. I smelled...something...we'll call it hyperbole. Meanwhile, Faisal had managed to retain possession of my actual passport.

We went home. Ate a sandwich. Cursed. Watched the clock tick down our chances of being able to go on the already planned, already booked vacation the following week.

And that's when the phone rang. My *iqama* was ready, and it and my passport were on my husband's desk at work.

Wait—*what?* You mean my *paperwork?* Ready for us to pick up so that we could meet Walid at the government office where he didn't work and yet that he would somehow force into operation?

Nope. The *iqama*. The finished, official, shiny card. Done. Sitting there as if it weren't made out of pure gold.

I don't know what happened. I never did. We drove to the office immediately, and when Dear Husband brought the card outside we could see that the picture was a photo of my passport picture, probably taken with a cell phone, probably emailed to a government worker with a wink and a nod and a reminder that *somebody* had hosted the Crown Prince in his home and knew people who could make your life better or worse. Or maybe it was emailed with a wink and a nod and a shared complaint about the kinds of guys who brag about hosting the Crown Prince in their home and how badly all us little guys would love to show them that *we're* the ones who actually get stuff done.

Fingerprint? I never got it. The blessing of voyage and a joyous residence resulted in no one ever asking me to put my finger to a reader.

And the lesson I learned? When it comes to expat interactions with officialdom, don't get too clever. Be as conventional as possible. You don't know what you don't know, and what you don't know can cause a world of trouble.

But there's more to it. Yes, what you know and what you

don't know will affect a lot of what happens as you move through expat life. I never knew the "whats" behind my *iqama* because there was zero chance I was going to risk that precious card by asking. Whatever happened definitely wasn't all by the book, but in some places the book is more open for interpretation than in others. A whole lot of "whats" I don't know, add up to a single "what" that I do: whatever works, works. For voyage, roll with it.

But it's also who (whom) you know, and the more of the population you know, everywhere, the better. The only way anything good happens in the whole world is by the "whos" taking care of each other. I'm pretty sure that particular "what" is the most important thing I'll ever know, and the only way to a joyous residence anywhere on earth.

22

MOMENTS AND MEMORIES - AKAJIULONNA PATRICIA NDEFO

Please list addresses and phone numbers for the past ten years.

They really can't be serious, I thought to myself. Like Santa, I checked it twice; in fact, I checked it three times. But I had read it correctly. The form I was completing, to pave the way for yet another career move, was requesting I provide my addresses and phone numbers over the past ten years... with zip codes!

You might be wondering what the fuss was about. Why was I sweating and laughing hysterically at the same time? It should be an easy enough task, right? Wrong! Now, if I had seen this form while growing up, or if my parents had to fill in such a form, it would have been a piece of cake. For me and a lot of my peers, we grew up at one address, at the most two. We went on holidays and we would always come "home" to that same address. In fact, not only do I still remember that home address, I remember our home phone number, my dad's office address and phone number, and my best friend's home phone number. It was that simple. Having lived there for so long, such information was engraved in your memory. That's just the way it was.

Fast forward to 2018: in the past ten years this form was enquiring about, I have had the wonderful opportunity to live on three out of our seven continents, make a home at eight addresses (four of which were in our "home" country, Nigeria), and use five different cellphone numbers, not to mention there were also landlines in all of this hullabaloo.

So, in my dazed state I went on to Facebook, because that is what you do in 2018, and called for help. Soon enough, some of my globetrotting friends bailed me out. If, like me, you do some online shopping on sites like Amazon, your shipping information is saved in your profile history. At least that was the case for me. I don't know if it is a setting, but Amazon saved my life.

Another savior would have been my dad. Daddy, while we were growing up, had this black address book which he always kept up to date. I would know because it was my job at some point to edit and fill in contact information in this book. With the arrival of cellphones or smartphones I later found out that my dad meticulously continued this tradition, only now it was my sister's job to update this information on his cellphone. My poor sister! At least my job was putting pen to paper; she had the joy of updating this information when cellphones were not so smart. Remember when moving the cursor meant painstakingly pressing left or right, and how tedious it was to get the alphabet right? In hindsight, I got off easy.

But you could always count on my dad to have my information saved over the years for every place where we have ever lived. Thinking of my dad brings me to one of the downsides of life on the move—time away from family.

Very early on this nomadic journey I realized my children would not have the conventional experiences that come with staying in one location and having family close by. They don't get sleepovers with the grandparents, aunties and uncles taking them out over the weekend and during school holidays, listening to folklore and stories of life in the "village" and the "olden" days, or enjoying huge family Sunday or holiday dinners. We tried our best to remedy this by always having the grandparents visit either during spring or summer every year, taking advantage of video calls, phone calls and all that social media had to offer. I will be quick to say it is never enough; but half a loaf, they say, is better than no loaf at all. I am definitely grateful for those precious moments.

I had my daughter while we were in the Netherlands. We had scheduled the family visits so that over her first eight months, we had some family member with us. It was the best decision ever! Daddy was around during Belle's fifth and sixth months. My dad changed diapers and fed my baby. He had always been an involved parent, but I cannot say he ever fed a baby or changed a diaper. However, while he was with us, and saw how I had to cope with going from having two nannies or housekeepers and a driver in Nigeria, to doing it all myself, he took it on. Daddy would babysit Belle while I went grocery shopping and ran errands, and when I'd get home, he would chase me off to go get some sleep. When I'd return or wake up, he would tell of how she woke up, he changed and fed her, the fun games they played, and some of the songs he sang to her... the same songs he and my mum sang to me and my siblings as babies. It was such a blessing having him there.

There were moments of Daddy telling the children tortoise folklore. Believe it or not, the tortoise is a very wise and often cunning creature in Igbo folklore. These stories were told with the hope of teaching morals, ethics and buttressing values, and with songs no less. I guess this was the 'Disney' of my Dad's generation.

Daddy and my trio would play Chinese checkers, The Game of Life, Stratego, and many of the other board games I played while growing up. It was fun to watch the children having the same zeal as I did, to want to beat Grandad at these games. Over our visits, Daddy has taught them hand games like *Sararamba*. When they play it now, it warms my heart because I know somehow, in all our up-and-away life-style, some things have been passed on and will stick around for yet another generation.

Daddy was to visit us in Calgary in the summer of 2018; however, he passed away before he could make that trip.

Being away from family is hard. However, I can confirm that being away and having a member of your family pass away is even harder. Absolutely nothing I have ever experienced compares with this. I remember the numbness. The guilt of not being closer, and with him. The sense of hopelessness and helplessness that I couldn't just board the next plane and head home to my dad. Nothing prepares you for this. For a while I was in a daze and thankful for my husband and good friends who helped watch the kids and ensure everything ran smoothly and I didn't lose my way.

Arriving in Nigeria that July, I felt like I received the news all over again. It felt more *real* somehow. Cue all the tears, anger, guilt and every emotion known on the planet. That summer in Nigeria, I felt or experienced them all. Nothing prepares you for losing a loved one while on an expatriate posting. No company delivers training, there are no workshops, or literature provided for *this*, as you decide to embark on your posting. Broaching this topic wasn't done. But maybe it should have been. I was in uncharted territory.

I questioned why I had to live so far away? Was an expatriate lifestyle really worth it? Could I not have stayed back with the children and let my husband go on the posting? But then I can hear my dad clearly, encouraging us always to enjoy every opportunity that presents itself. He himself was also well-travelled as a diplomat, in business and for leisure. He always advised us to make the most of every opportunity and find ways to make it work for us. It was a joy sharing stories, similarities, and changes in cities we had both lived in or visited.

If I can share any advice, it's this advice passed down from my dad: expatriate living, though life-altering in every way, is definitely not all shopping for designer apparel, lounging by the pool sipping coffee or wine, and having maids wait on you hand and foot. Far from it! What it is, is an opportunity for you to embark on a journey and enjoy experiences that will enrich you and make your life so much fuller. It pushes you to step away from your comfort zone and birth a stronger you. Though away from friends and family, be intentional at keeping in touch. Call as often as you can and as often as you remember them; drop a text, do video calls, make silly videos, have them over for a weekend, a holiday, or even an extended stay. Be intentional in encouraging the passing down of traditions. Trust me, they will be great keepsakes for when loved ones leave this earth.

The pain of losing a loved one is great. It is even more crippling when you are miles and miles away. Allow yourself to grieve. Give expression to what you feel and allow yourself to heal.

We are currently in our fifth "home" country which was also where my dad served as Consul General. The apple doesn't fall too far from the tree I suppose. It would have been awesome to have him visit us here, share moments, and make memories. I guess I will do that with him forever in my heart.

I know I will come to love this new city and country as he did. While I am it, I best make sure I update my growing list of our global contact information.

23

I BLEW UP MY HAIRDRYER TODAY - JENNIFER ROBINSON, PH.D.

Yes, you read that title right. I hear this is a rather common experience for those of us who use US-specification hairdryers, with allegedly inadequate voltage, overseas. Yes, I DID buy the adaptor, so it does not account for a sudden surge of 220 volts of electricity through a device that should only handle 110 volts of electricity. Let's just say that I said a very fast prayer, gently unplugged the smoking machine that turned a shade of orange I never knew a hairdryer could be, and, with arms sticking as far away from my body as possible, took it to the innkeepers. "Um...my hairdryer just blew up when I plugged it in. It is still hot and smoking. Can you take it from me?"

I love to travel. In my youth, I traveled quite a bit. I was born into the army, lived overseas, moved back to the States, my parents divorced, and I became a Midwest-Southwest traveling custody kid. One parent stayed in the army and the other moved back to her home town. By ninth grade, I had attended nine schools in two different countries. This might sound stressful, but, according to my current supervisors, I have crazy adaptability skills and adjust to change easily (I now add that to every single resume). So, when my husband, who works for the US Government, came home and asked if I wanted to move to England or Germany, I was more concerned about how the military would move my entire house. Not just the stuff *in* my house, but my entire house. I loved that house. We had just settled in three years before and were not ready to move any place else. Yet, we were already moving again. This time it was overseas.

I had not lived overseas since I was much younger. I have moved all over the US and even did a teaching exchange in Japan (ask me about that story over a glass of wine!), but now I was moving a full house, three kids, three animals, and my job overseas. Whether I was ready to be an expat or not, it was happening.

By the end of October we were living in England, in a pub. Yup, that is a normal thing. In the US, we call them bed and breakfasts, but I much preferred to tell my friends and family that the US government was paying for me to live in a pub. It sounded more adventurous. The pub had been the home of a very well-known historical figure from the 1400s. I think the steep incline up three flights of stairs and the lack of elevator was proof that this was a very old building. If nothing else, the squeak of every floorboard was a reminder. This pub was my home for about three weeks. By the end of our stay, we were often greeted with, "Oy! It's the Americans!"

I learned so many things.

First of all, I have an accent – well, at least according to the very sweet and handsome Romanian bartender, who would flirtatiously remind me of my supposed accent. He loved how I said bA-con instead of ba-cOn and how I said faLAfel, instead of falaFEL. He loved to repeat my words with my accent. I did not have the heart to tell this very young and boisterous person that he was the one with the accent. Since tipping is not a common thing and I was at least 20 years his senior, I just surmised that he enjoyed teasing me about my accent. I now say falaFEL, but still say bAcon.

Second, I hate roundabouts. There are two types of people in the world: those who love roundabouts and those, the intelligent ones like me, who have a disdain for round-abouts. I have never seen anything so confusing in my life while driving. Imagine, if you will, your local roundabout with five lanes, four sets of stoplights, seven exits, and a never-ending circle. Just for fun, let's connect two of them. Who did not have enough to do in the day to plan a double roundabout?! For fun, let's add driving on the left side of the road and navigating being on the right side of the car (the driver's side in the UK). I am amazed that there are not daily pile-ups! Learning to drive with my kids in the car took linguistic self-control that I did not know I possessed.

Third, before becoming a pedestrian in another country, good luck understanding the rules, because no one will tell you them! A smart person will remember that learning to drive on the left side of the road means that *everyone* drives on the left side of the road. So, when attempting to cross the street, it is possible to be nearly hit by a bus, cause a great deal of honking to happen, and have people shake their heads at you if you look the wrong way and then cross. Look right *then* left…and then right and left…then once more, right and left; not the opposite. But, wait! There is a twist! Busses can go in the opposite direction to cars on some streets. So, looking right *then* left is grand until there are roads where the busses go left to right just off the sidewalk (or pavement), while in the next lane cars travel right to left, and in the lane after that cars travel left to right. It is like a live-action game of Frogger! The bus still did not hit me, so I am not sure what all the fuss was about. Never mind, give me the car keys. I'll drive eight blocks to find parking after driving two blocks to the store. I'll go through the countryside to avoid the roundabouts.

The best thing about traveling is learning a new language. It is possible to learn a phrase or word that is better than anything in your native language, even if the native language is technically the same as the language in your new home country. My favorites include:

Bays – parking spots…makes complete sense!

Flu jab – no explanation needed for those who are already terrified of shots.

Half 8 – 8:30…this one still makes me think.

Faff – to waste time doing nothing in particular or nothing useful

Petrol is for a car and *gas* is for a stove.

A *backyard* is the concrete area directly behind a house; the *garden* is the grassy area behind the house.

Pudding – dessert. If you want US-style pudding, I am not sure what to say.

Lemonade is Sprite or 7Up or something similar. I am not sure how to ask for US-style lemonade.

However, the *absolutely* best part of traveling is being

able to see history as it might have looked 1000, or even 2000, years ago. Where we live now, we can touch the walls of Roman forts and walk the halls of a 600-year-old priory (a small monastery or abbey). There's the opportunity to meet new people who think in different ways. Who would we be without the ability to travel, both in the past and in the modern day?

It is also possible to meet your soulmate while traveling. Be careful; it might not be who you are envisioning. My soulmate is a near-elderly British woman who made my husband march back to the car and straighten up in the bay. She told him that there was no reason for him to park in such a way and if he was going to be living in England, then he would need to learn to stay in the bay. To my surprise, my 47-year-old, combat-veteran husband laughed nervously, said, "Yes, ma'am," and got back into that car to straighten up! While he was in the car, she winked at me and said that she had been looking forward to a day in her life when she could bother a man about his driving and make him listen. I know she and I will meet in another life.

I can replace the hairdryer. What I can't replace are those unique experiences that make the cost of a fried appliance so worthwhile.

24

THE OVERNIGHT TRAIN TO LIUZHOU - ROBIN BLANC

It's 8:29 in the evening and I'm sitting on a lower bunk in a sleeper train in China: from Guangzhou to Liuzhou, to be exact. This journey won't be over until the morning when we arrive in Liuzhou at 8:10 tomorrow morning. I pull out my laptop and start writing.

Today started with me staying up late to take advantage of the internet in Hong Kong and finish my binge-watching of *Stranger Things*. I fell asleep around 2am during a 'Behind the Scenes' episode. My alarm woke me at 8am for my 10am appointment at the Chinese Embassy in Hong Kong to pick up my passport and new work visa. I had a bottle of orange juice and two bananas for breakfast, thinking I would grab lunch after the embassy, and before I started the trip home.

Laughable, in retrospect.

I packed up the last few things into my bags and headed off to the embassy. From the hotel in Wan Chai, I had to walk about half a mile to get there.

I arrived at 9:30 and there was already a long line of

people, but not nearly as many as the day before, when I had dropped off my application. We waited until 10am when they opened the door. There was a mad rush to be first at the elevators, or 'lifts' as they call them in Hong Kong. Then there was another dash upstairs to get into the line to pay. It wasn't too long of a line and it moved fairly quickly. But the woman at the window told me that it was cash only. *How did I forget what I'd been told the day before?*

She told me the nearest ATM was downstairs. So I went downstairs and located the Bank of China. This was where my problems really began. I went in and attempted to withdraw enough to pay the ransom for my passport, but got a slip telling me I had insufficient funds. Since it was the end of the month, and I had paid $300US for an extra night in the hotel so I could shop, and I *had* shopped, as well as buying a train ticket from Guangzhou to Hong Kong, I was low on funds. I'd be reimbursed when I returned, but it made things tight!

I assessed the situation. I already had almost enough cash to pay for my visa, so all I really needed was the balance and a bit to pay the taxi to the station. I tried again and got the money. Crisis averted, I took solace in knowing I would get paid at the beginning of the month, along with getting reimbursed.

Back at the embassy, I paid and got my receipt so that I could stand in another line, much longer, to pick up my passport. My boredom was eased by getting to know another American in the line who was also teaching in China.

I got my passport with the new visa and walked back to the hotel. The night before, after asking for advice at the front desk, I had been advised to leave at noon for my 13:11

train, to allow for lunch hour traffic. She assured me that they'd get me a cab. It was just after 11:00, so I decided I had time to go two blocks to Marks & Spencer. They had a nice little gluten-free section with fresh bread. I was going to hand-carry it all the way home if I had to, but I'd been dreaming of bread for two months!

I bought the bread, and made it back to the hotel by 11:45am. I went upstairs, packed the bread in a stiff paper shopping bag with a couple of folded city maps on the sides to protect it, then placed it in the top of my backpack where it had the best chance of not getting smooshed. I headed downstairs with my packed bags and checked out. Easy peasy.

Or so it seemed.

The woman who went outside to flag down a cab couldn't get one to stop. When she finally did, they refused to drive to the other side of the harbor. *Tick tick tick.* Ten minutes became fifteen minutes. I spoke with another staff member who explained that lunch time was a busy time. I explained that this was why I had made a point of asking the night before so that I could be sure to have a cab at the time I needed. He apologized. Twenty minutes had gone by now. Two men who had just checked out were helped into a cab that stopped a couple of minutes later. I was shocked. The hotel worker with me explained again that cabs did not want to cross the harbor.

I anxiously pointed out that my train left at 13:11 and it was now 12:25. At that point he finally seemed to comprehend my anxiety and ran out to the woman outside. They finally managed to flag a taxi just after 12:30. The man told the driver that I was late, and the driver made a valiant effort, but the traffic was jammed. As soon as he pulled up to the train station, I jumped out and started running.

I got inside to the boarding area. The woman there got agitated and ran over to the desk to try to get me on the train, but the person at the desk said no. It was just a couple of minutes after 1pm.

Stress.

I had missed my train, and I had two more trains to catch to get home! I texted the school where I worked to see if they could help, and went to see about getting on the next train.

The woman told me I couldn't transfer the ticket. I had to buy a new one. I'd just spent the last of my money on the visa.

More stress.

I had to sit down and think over my options. I managed to find an open chair in a waiting area where I could calm down. With relief, I remembered that I had stashed some US money in my bag when I flew to Beijing two months before. I found it, and went to the exchange to get Hong Kong Dollars (HKD). I returned to the ticket window and got a ticket for the next train. Crisis averted, again.

In the pre-departure waiting area, I met a very nice Brazilian woman who let me use her mobile hotspot so that I could keep texting back to school to find out what to do. They told me that I should be able to make the next train, but that it would be close. I texted my college friend who lived in Guangzhou and asked for his help. As I boarded the train, I got his reply. Unfortunately, he had a meeting and couldn't meet me. I decided I would take a taxi instead of the subway once I got to Guangzhou.

But first, on arrival in Guangzhou, I had to get past immigration. Before the train had even stopped, people were up and had their bags ready. Since I knew I had a tight connection, I joined them. After disembarking, I got into a line that was slightly shorter than the rest and waited. It seemed like the other lines were moving faster, but not much. After a while, the transit police told us to go over into the Chinese-only lanes, since all the local people had gone through.

Of course everyone sprinted over, and by the time I got there I was last. The line was only about six people and it moved fairly quickly, but I was one of the last to get through. Outside the station there were guys asking if I needed a taxi, but when they saw my ticket, they just said *meiyou, meiyou,* (which means no, no) and pointed to the time. It was half an hour to departure and there was no way I was going to make it, because the next train left from the *other* train station across town.

I couldn't believe how badly my journey was going.

Eventually I found one driver who spoke a bit of English. I told him I would go to the other station, hoping I could exchange the ticket. Since I was again unable to get a signal, he let me use his phone to call Carol, my contact at school. She talked with the taxi driver in Chinese about what I needed to do. When they finished, Carol told me that the taxi driver would help me get a new ticket, on an overnight sleeper train, and drive me to the other station. Another new ticket? Overnight train?

Things couldn't possibly get any worse.

I still had some HKD, so he took me to the exchange window and I converted everything I had back to yuan. It was *just* enough to buy the new ticket and pay 100 yuan to the driver. Of course at the ticket window there was a mob of people. He just went right up and got in front of everyone and was able to get the ticket. Then he hustled me out to the taxi and got me to the other station, but had to let me out a block away because of traffic.

I followed everyone else into an outdoor screening area, with x-ray machines for bags. There was so much pushing and shoving, especially as they only let people through one at a time. Just as I was within range of the scanner, the guards opened up the gate and let everyone through. I followed along and went to the actual entrance to the station to stand in line again. Once I got though, I was tapped on the shoulder and told to bring my bags to a table for inspection.

Really?

The woman went through my bag like she was looking for something specific. She pulled out the salt grinder I'd bought at Marks & Spencer and wanted to know what it was. I just looked at her and said 'salt!' I didn't even have the energy to grab my phone for Google Translate. She finished and motioned for me to go. And I skedaddled because the guy next to me was pulling out an arsenal from his bag, including lots of knives and a meat cleaver.

I found the departure lounge, and then only had to wait for about five minutes before people headed to the platform. Of course my car was the next to last one, at the end of the train. I was *so* tired and was trying to run because the platform was getting emptier and emptier and I did NOT want to miss another train!

I finally made it on board. There was a long line of bunks

and I was too frazzled to try to figure out which one was mine. A man looked at my ticket and motioned me down the rows to the correct bunk. I was so happy it was on the bottom, because they were stacked three high! I sat down and shoved my carry-on bag underneath. I pulled the other bag close and just rested while I tried to catch my breath.

We seemed to be sitting for a while so I decided to find the bathroom at the end of the car. It was locked. It didn't get unlocked until after the train was moving. Maybe they were worried about stowaways. We finally set off, I got to visit the toilet, and rinse off my dirty stained hands. I was very happy that I had bought a packet of Dettol wipes in Hong Kong. Back at my bunk, I disinfected my hands and pulled out the bread and cheese I'd bought at M&S. A woman came by with a cart of drinks. I had a 5 yuan coin left in my pocket, so I was able to get two waters.

The other passengers had either bought food at the station, or had come prepared. Some had instant cup-o-noodles that they filled from the hot water dispenser. A few were smoking. But at least I was finally able to stop moving. I had felt like a perpetual motion machine for most of the day. I didn't feel like reading, so here I am, with my laptop, writing the whole miserable story.

At 9:30 the train stops and picks up more passengers. I keep typing.

Then a man walks by, stops, comes back, passes again, and finally sits on the bunk next to mine – only two feet away! Holy moly. It hadn't occurred to me that a guy would be sleeping within reaching distance.

I keep typing, trying to come to terms with this new twist.

Well, he is fully clothed and so am I. I'll concentrate on my writing.

Or not....

At 10:00 the steward comes down the aisle and barks at me to lay down, motioning so I'll know what he means. And then the lights go out.

I try to keep typing but the glare is irritating. I put away the laptop and pull out my Kindle to read, but the darkness combined with my exhaustion means that I fall asleep pretty quickly.

But I don't get to stay asleep. The train stops several times to let people on and off.

And the guy two feet away snores.

He does get off the train at some point, and in the morning I wake up alone in my little alcove. The woman with the cart comes back and I try to buy another water with a 5 yuan coin I've found in my bag, but now it costs 10 yuan!

I do get to see a beautiful sunrise before the train arrives in Liuzhou. Carol comes to get me since I am now totally broke and can't afford a taxi. I get back to school just in time to go teach my morning class.

The overnight train to Liuzhou was certainly a journey to remember!

25

THE SECOND WIFE - SHIRLEY PREVOST

"I'm the second wife."

The words take me by surprise. I'm trying to control my poker face. I repeat to myself silently: *relax, keep calm and don't be judgemental.*

So many questions are buzzing around in my head! I have been secretly waiting for this moment to happen since I was introduced to one of my husband's friends eight months ago. "What do you mean this man needs three cell phones, lives with two different wives, and has families in two different houses at the same time?" I asked my husband at the time.

Polygamy was quite a strange reality for me as a Canadian.

This beautiful and charming Emirati woman, dressed just like me to attend a friend's BBQ, couldn't have said more to destabilize me. Dubai, my new homeland of two years, was all about camels, desert heat, sandstorms, world-renowned 6-star hotels, luxury cars, famous skyscrapers, and futuristic obsessions to reach the top...not polygamy! To be honest, before that evening, I literally knew nothing about it.

Polygamous relationships are legal in the United Arab Emirates, and according to Sharia law, a Muslim man may have four wives. Most Emirati men have just one wife, but roughly a quarter are known to have a second wife. It's even more uncommon to have a third or fourth wife, yet perfectly legal. Sheikh Mohammed bin Rashid Al Maktoum, Vice President of the UAE and ruler of Dubai, has six wives and a total of 23 children.

My current reality is that 'Wife #2' is standing in front of me and my curiosity is piqued. I have to tread carefully. I'm so curious, but I don't want to cross any lines and be disrespectful; she is a stranger after all.

Surprisingly, she is very pleased to explain her reality. Hers was a love story guided by her core values and principles. She was just following a different path than mine to get the same goal: love and happiness, no matter which religion is followed. I thoroughly enjoy our fascinating conversation, learning about polygamous relationships.

First, men need valid reasons to have multiple wives. If a man's first wife was unable to have children, but the man wanted to have a family, this would be an acceptable reason. Polygamous men have to look after each wife materially and treat them equally. Can you imagine having to afford two households at the same time? It's expensive! The Emirati government supports this situation, with the goal of increasing the population of native Emirati. With this being said, an Emirati earns up to 25% more salary than any expat for the same job.

The husband must split his nights equally among his wives and he should live in equal homes. A 4000-square-foot home for Wife #1 means a 4000-square-foot home for Wife #2! Each wife receives an equal allowance for each child under her care. The same applies to vacations, nights out and gifts.

If the husband struggles to choose gifts for his loved one...can you imagine the challenge for two wives? I suppose that's where they can take advantage of their situation. A polygamous man can shop with Wife #2 to get gifts for Wife #1. That's likely to be a successful strategy because if you remember: $10000 of gold jewellery for Wife #1 means $10000 of gold jewellery for Wife #2! It seems like a win-win for everyone!

My tongue is burning to ask a crucial question.

"Are you jealous?"

"Of course! I'm human!" is her answer. After all, basic human feelings are the same!

After the party, I return home full of gratitude. I can't stop thinking how lucky I am to have met this amazing woman. That's what I love about my expat life: the opportunity to have a sneak peek into others' realities.

It's through talking, love, compassion and leaving judgement behind that this world can be a better place.

26

FINDING HOME - ASHLY JEANDEL

"...the biggest lesson I have learned is that sometimes we have to leave home, our house, our village, or our country, in order to grow, and to understand who we are..."

"Boarding for gate H to Dublin. Boarding for gate H to Dublin," I heard from overhead. I peeked up from my book to see the long line forming. My eyes wandered over to the people in that line. The father holding his little girl with pigtails, while she played with the curls on the back of his head. The daughter helping her stiff elderly father to the plane. I wished I had made it to that point, helping my Father in his old age. The flight attendant checked my passport and my boarding pass. I boarded the plane and sat down in my window seat. I stared out of the window and my thoughts took me back to my life on the farm. Back to when I was a carefree nineteen-year-old girl in college, before I lost my dad.

It happened so fast and so unexpectedly. My father was

farming one day and felt a pain in his lower stomach. It was so painful he fell to one knee. One second he was standing there in the field, then the next he had disappeared into it. That is when I got the phone call. I was living in Toronto, Canada at the time. My father told me it would be okay; that he was getting tests done and he assured me it was nothing. I wish I could go back to the day before that phone call, the days when I didn't know that kind of pain.

A few days later they flew me back to Manitoba, my uncle picking me up at the airport. I knew it was bad, and I still have flashbacks of that day. My aunt told me in her living room. I can remember the crushing feeling of my knees hitting their wood flooring and the immediate need to vomit. My father was terminally ill with colon cancer and had months left to live. The next months were spent sitting on hospital floors, enduring cancer treatments and sickness.

Sometimes my dad would ask the difficult questions, about the future. I would answer him as best as I could and then disappear to somehow accept this was my reality. He had dreams he never got to live out. Our family has Swedish roots and it was his dream to one day return to Sweden and see the land that our ancestors had farmed. He made me promise that I would go. He said he would be in Valhalla soon, so it was up to me to go. We also spoke about the day that I would get married and how I would play a certain song and save that dance for him. He asked how many children I wanted to have ; I told him two, a girl and a boy. "Fingers crossed!" he said. We laughed and cried and hugged, and tried to hold onto every last moment together. After a short three-month battle with the disease, the end was near.

My father wanted to die in the same village he grew up in, that he got married in, and had his children in. He wanted to be in the community that supported him and that he loved. The day came when he was moved from the cancer treatment hospital to our local hospital. It happened when I was sitting beside him. He was surrounded by family, when I saw his chest stop moving up and down. I knew. We all knew, our Viking was gone.

As we were walking out of the hospital I saw the two suited-up men from the funeral home, coming to take my father's body for cremation. I couldn't mentally take on that next step and tried my best to ignore them. As we walked outside we could see the Canada geese flying over and there was a mist that had settled over the prairies and my heart.

I knew it then, that I wouldn't see those Canada geese for a long time. After settling the estate, selling the family farm, and finishing college I needed to breath. I felt suffocated with responsibility and I had always had a sense of adventure that was just itching to be scratched. I had a deep need to change, to leave, to find who I was in this new life. Part of me knew that I was running away, however I also knew that it was time to fulfil that promise that I made to my Dad.

I packed my backpack. I left. I bought a one-way ticket to Ireland, by myself, ready to be a different me. To be where people didn't know me, where I could escape my reality and figure out who I was without my dad. In the end I found memories, or things that reminded me of him, everywhere I went.

After months of traveling around Europe I bought the ticket to Sweden. When I arrived at the airport, the customs officer read my name out loud, LARSON, Ashly. With a half smile, he said, well, "Welcome home Miss. "

I spent a couple weeks researching my family roots which led me to a small village in the middle of nowhere. There was a small lake, with a bridge crossing part of it, and a church. My ancestors were farmers who left Sweden for new adventures in Canada (must be where I got my adventurous side from). I was able to see the clergy books and see when they got married and a line through their names when they left for America. I was walking around the outside of the little church when an older, blonde-haired lady came and asked me if I wanted to go inside.

She lived near the church and told me to take as long as I needed. After thanking her I opened the heavy wooden doors and emotion hit me like a tidal wave. The church was decorated in yellow, and blue, and gold. I cracked a smile. My father used to paint everything in yellow and blue, even the fences at our farm. I touched each pew lightly as I walked down the aisle. I sat in the front pew and cried. I cried and cried for what felt like hours. It was a release that I hadn't expected. Painful and yet at the same time freeing. I never imagined that returning to my roots while on an adventure would lead me to this kind of understanding of grief and who I was.

When my father was cremated my siblings and I all got a small wooden box with some of his ashes in it. After leaving the church, I walked down the winding path to the lake. I walked halfway over the bridge, leaned over the side, and I emptied the box into the lake. Finally, in one way, my father, my Viking, made it home and had one last adventure.

After this promise was fulfilled I felt free and light and realised that I was who I was because of my father. It was time for me to learn and grow by myself and to let new people into my life. He was part of me now, no matter where I lived in the world.

I continued to travel and took a job in eastern France as a Nanny (au pair). When I was working in this small French village I met the love of my life. Twelve years later I still live in the same small village. I have found my community here, my people who love and support me. I have realised that living as an expat can be difficult and I have hundreds of stories of misunderstandings, language, or cultural difficulties.

However, the biggest lesson I have learned from living overseas is that sometimes we have to leave home, our families, our village, or our country, in order to grow, and to understand who we are. Our souls are so much more than where we live; it is that, and a combination of the people who have come into and left our lives.

And I did fulfil one more promise to my father. My husband and I have two beautiful children: one boy and one girl.

27

WHERE IN THE WORLD ARE YOU FROM? - DIANA BOND

"Where are you from?" is one of the most challenging questions my kids could be asked. Doing so usually results in an expression of bewilderment and a sinking feeling of having to make a split-second decision: to respond with the short answer or the long one. The short answer will depend entirely on which country they are in when the question is asked. If in Australia, the response will be "Canada" or "England". If in Canada, it might be "England" or "Australia". Or it might be: "Well, I have passports from Australia, England and Canada." Then again, that sounds a bit pretentious, so better pick one... If, however, the asker genuinely sounds interested, my child will say something to this effect: "Well, since my parents are British and Canadian, I have citizenship from both countries. However, I was born in Turkey, went to kindergarten in Korea, attended preschool in Hong Kong, did my elementary and middle school years in Thailand (by which time the asker has taken on a peculiar glazed expression) and finished high school in Australia, where I also have citizenship. I am now attending university in Canada." End of conversation.

In a nutshell, that explains one of my most challenging goals as an expatriate mother: how to navigate the minefields of life on the move in such a way as to create a sense of 'belonging' for our family. The reality is that 'home' is where we are planted—for the time being. Redefining our definition of 'home' and 'normal' changes every few years, as we try to embrace a new reality, find new friends, and adjust to a new way of thinking.

The question that leaves *me* in a heap of indecision is: "Which country did you enjoy living in the most?" How on earth do I answer that? Do I settle for the exoticism and foreignness of Saudi Arabia, the food and customs of Japan, the hospitality and bustle of Istanbul, the lights and action of Hong Kong, the incredibly supportive expat community in Seoul, or the intrigue and ancient/modern blend of Bangkok? As I'm left stuttering and trying to explain all this without sounding arrogant, I usually end up with a version of, "Oh, they all had their pros and cons."

The life of an expat is one of the most diverse, challenging, exciting, frustrating, and loneliest in the world. The opportunities we have had, to explore ancient cultures, learn traditional customs, experience tantalising tastes, and meet an amazing diversity of people, are incomparable. We have been scuba diving in the Red Sea, watched the sunrise from the top of Mount Fuji, explored the ancient ruins of Cappadocia, crisscrossed the Masai Mara, snorkelled on the Great Barrier Reef, stood atop the Great Wall of China, and kayaked with killer whales. While most kids were collecting postage stamps, mine were collecting passport stamps. Ah yes, you say—what a glamorous lifestyle! Maids, drivers, travel—what more could you want?

The trade-off is a choice we have had to live with. We have experienced more grief in 20 years than most people will experience in a lifetime. Life on the move means saying good-bye to friends every one to three years on average—if we aren't moving, they are. Because of the separation from family, and knowing friendships are short-term, we have learned to make friends quickly and deeply. There is no time for the 'getting to know you' phase where you can gradually get to know someone and determine whether or not to pursue the relationship. As an expat, it's all or nothing.

This caused difficulties when transitioning to Australia, the country we eventually embraced as 'home'. My daughter's new friends had known each other for years, and weren't ready for an outsider who wanted to know everything about them in two hours or less. She had travelled the world but couldn't navigate the local bus system. She didn't know any of the TV serials that were part of lunchtime conversations. Her new friends imagined Bangkok as mud shacks with grass roofs and dirt floors. How could she explain the exquisite lifestyle and state of the art school when that wasn't in their frame of reference? She had to learn the hard way that transitioning is lonely. We learn not to talk about our past and instead to survive in the present. Added to that, maintaining friendships long-term was much harder—they (or us) didn't leave when we discovered all their idiosyncrasies! We couldn't just 'move on' and start afresh.

But despite the struggles, I would never trade in those

years of cross-cultural living. What we missed on some levels, we gained in others. We have learned to be adaptable. We have learned to embrace diversity of culture, skin colour and beliefs. What an eye-opener when my kids described their new friends not by the colour of their eyes or hair, but by their personality and character. We have learned to be global citizens, and that our western worldview is not always the right one. We have learned that there is so much on this journey of life that we can't 'teach' our children. It must be felt. It must be tasted. It must be experienced.

I am thankful that in this day of modern technology, we are better able to keep in touch with the friends who have passed through our lives. At the end of the day, it isn't where we've been or what we've seen that's changed us—it's the people we have met and shared life with for even a short time who have irrevocably left imprints on our souls and changed us forever. We value and treasure those who have become family, and though they, too, have moved on, we have shared a part of ourselves that no one who's 'never been there' can understand. We have shared hurts, victories, losses and celebrations with those who have become family, because we couldn't do it with our own. My greatest joy is having the opportunity to catch up with an old friend, when, even though many years and many miles may separate us, we can pick up where we left off, not because we have kept in touch over the years, but because we 'understand' each other. We don't have to explain ourselves, and we don't have to apologise—we can just be who we have grown to be.

Life on the move has also taught me to seize opportunities when they arise, because they may not come again. As a result, I have done many things I would never have dreamt possible and recognise the value of the transferable skills I have picked up along the way. Those skills have enabled me to be creative, persistent and diplomatic in many areas of life. They've also given me the courage to take on challenges that surprise even myself. I mean, how many people do you know who are doing a PhD at the *end* of their working life?

And where are we now? Well, we managed to get our kids through high school in our adopted country. They in turn have studied, travelled and are individually trying to assimilate who they are as Third Culture Kids into their new roles as young adults in an ever-changing world.

As for my husband and myself, well, we are on the move again! We have seized the opportunity to do some mission work in Thailand, so we are back 'home' in a sense, having spent the longest span of our expat life in this country. The sights are familiar, the smells are familiar, the language is familiar; our roles are different. But we have adapted well and are enjoying our new status. We are content. We know that we are exactly where we are meant to be—for now.

28

ROAD TRIPPING - KENDRA DAVIDSON

Diplomats are strange kinda birds. Always ready for the next adventure, half out the door, and always prepared for any disaster. My parents were the ultimate adventurers, so, when looking back, it is not a surprise that I had some crazy experiences. Including a road trip from hell.

I am not sure my parents really told me about our summer plans. I think the movers showed up, packed the house, and I just found myself at the age of seven, in a gold Ford LTD in the '80s, surrounded by pillows and the stench of burritos, in the middle of a sweltering summer. My father had decided we were going to drive from Mexico City to Ottawa, Canada. Why? Because I believe he just thought it would be cool, because all road trips with seven-year-olds in the desert sun are fun, right? After living abroad for six years (three in China, three in Mexico), we were finally moving back to Ottawa, known in the diplomatic circle as headquarters. The hitch: my brother and sister, who were teens, got to fly off to BC to hang out with my grandparents; even our family dog got to fly right to Ottawa to spend two weeks with my great-aunt and uncle; and there I was, the seven-year-old who was left behind to be dragged on a road trip.

Back then, the roads from Mexico City to the US border were rough; by rough, I mean there weren't that many actual roads, just dirt tracks mixed in with dry dirt roads, with Mexican food stalls scattered here and there; some were semi-paved, some went through nothing but cacti, and then a paved road would just appear out of nowhere. The heat was so intense, everything on the horizon blurred into waves. My mother would quietly shove Gravol into me; between the weather and the motion sickness, I was a hot mess to travel with. I'm not sure why they thought this drive was a good idea, but parents don't do rational things, especially not the adventurous ones I had. I mean, my mother kept toilet paper in the glove compartment "just in case." And my father travelled with a mini emergency medicine kit.

The moment we left our empty house in Mexico City, I was shoved in the back seat of that Ford LTD. The car was so big, you couldn't fit the whole car into a single frame of a picture. The backseat was so bouncy that I am pretty sure the seatbelt was meant to keep you from bouncing out of the car and had nothing to do with crash safety. I was squished in the back, surrounded by pillows and blankets. My mother attempted to make it as comfortable as possible, but I never understood the blankets; it was 100 degrees back there, I wasn't about to get hypothermia. In between Gravol naps, I would lean in as close to my father's ear as possible, and ask, "are we there yet?" and "how much longer?" My father claimed I started asking about two minutes after we left our house in Mexico, and then promptly asked every hour, on the hour, the whole two weeks it took to drive. I doubted that claim until I had to go on a road trip with my seven-year-old, and I am pretty sure 'every hour' is being generous.

I slipped in and out of a dream state. The landscape was nothing new to me, nor were the trucks packed with workers, and random people hanging out of them holding chickens or bundles of flowers to sell, or the heavily-armed guards at specific checkpoints; it was home. I had no comprehension that life across two borders would be vastly different.

As we slowly neared the US border, I remember being very alert, very curious as to what lay ahead. The border looked like nothing I had ever seen. It was new and shiny. My father pulled out our diplomatic passports and handed them to the border patrol. The man looked stern at first, curious about the crazy diplomatic family bumping along to the border. "Where have you come from?" the border control officer asked. My father replied, "Mexico City, we are driving back to Ottawa."

The border patrol officer's face broke into a relaxed smile, and he replied, "Are you nuts? You drove from Mexico City to here, and you plan on going further north?"

Long road trips were not the norm in those days, especially driving across North America. There was no GPS, and heck, my father hadn't even booked hotels along the way. We were winging it! Whatever motel he saw with a pool at around 2pm, would be the place we would stop for the night. The drive through Mexico's border towns wasn't as dangerous as they are today, but they were rough. My father knew Mexico, knew the language and culture; he didn't think he was crazy, he just wanted to cross another adventure off his bucket list.

As we crossed the border, things were visibly different. It was a difference I had never seen or experienced. I had spent three years in China and three in Mexico. I had yet to remember what Canada looked like, and this was my first time on US soil. As we drove, the roads were dusty; you could see the oil rigs in the distance. The smell of corn tortillas, burritos and beans disappeared and was replaced with rubber, oil and heat that made you woozy. There was nothing to see. As we got closer to a city, my father turned into a motel, the kind that was popular in the '50s, but had decayed over time. We drove up to the white three-storied building with the doors of the rooms facing outward, painted a bright aqua, but peeling a bit from being painted in the heat. The structure was U-shaped, and there was a pool in the middle. The building itself was not of interest to me, nope: I saw the famous golden arches across the way. I had seen a couple of commercials on a new American channel we got in Mexico, and I wanted to go. I had never had a 'real' burger or at least one my father hadn't made and broken a tooth on. So I begged my father to go to McDonald's. My mother was not keen; she was the original 'organic and wholegrain' mum. We had six years of no fast food— heck, I didn't even know what that was, I just wanted McDonald's. I wore my parents down; they finally agreed, but only after I spent a couple of hours swimming and letting my father nap. At dinner time, we headed to McDonald's, and I was beyond excited; I couldn't wait to tell my sister and brother that I got to have McDonald's. Little did I know, they were getting Dairy Queen and my grandmother's excellent food.

My mother, a closet fast food fan (she just never liked to admit it) wolfed hers down; my father took his time. I ate mine like a wild dog, terrified my parents would take it away from me. I don't even think I breathed in the smell or the taste, it just went down in one gulp.

We headed back to our motel, and within 15 minutes, our McDonald's didn't agree with us. Not like, I-have-a-stomachache kinda ill, but like, the-taps-are-open-I'm-going-to-die kinda ill. My mother kept muttering that we had left the dirtiest city in the world and survived every single illness, and here we were in the US and we got struck with the nastiest food poisoning at a fast food restaurant; it was somewhat ironic. I'm not sure how we survived that night, especially with one bathroom, but we did, and my father kept to our 5am departure the next day. We were back on the road a little rough around the edges, but we were keeping food down, and I was back to a semi-conscious Gravol state of mind.

Then, like our stomachs giving out, our car had to have her turn. She gave out on the side of the road, and I woke up eating dust in a pool of perspiration and with a pillow stuck to my head, my father swearing in several different languages, my mother dancing around pretending this was part of the whole adventure. My father had to arrange for a tow truck to bring it to the nearest garage. The only plus, when the tow truck arrived, was that we got to sit in the tow truck, and I got to have a candy bar out of the vending machine at the garage; I was pretty satisfied with that outcome. We were then dropped off at another motel. My father broke it to us that we would have to be there for a few days. Back then, my father had to hang out at the garage with a book all day, because there was no way to reach him and relay what needed to be done to the car.

My mother, on the other hand, decided that while my father hung out at the garage, we were going to head to a mall. A MALL! I was seven, and I had no idea what a mall was. At least, not the American version of a mall, and goodness, there was no such thing as a mall in China.

The moment we stepped in, the cold air hit me. The shiny, beautiful floors sparkled; the glittering lights above the stores, the smell of pretzels...it was like nothing I had ever seen or imagined. My mother, hiding her shock, took my hand and said, "Let's go here."

So we wandered through the mall and ended up at the ice-cream counter. As my mother ordered, she almost burst into tears; it had been the first time she had ordered anything in English in six years. She was in shock. I looked at the young man scooping my ice-cream; in my pretty thick Mexican accent I said, "Hey, you speak English!" The poor kid looked bewildered; I was blonde and blue-eyed, and wasn't supposed to have a thick accent. He must have thought we had come from the woods, or we had just left a commune. He gave me the oddest look and nodded.

We took our ice-cream and sat down; the hum of machines, the hustle and bustle of the people, the rustling of shopping bags, was all new and surprising. I was in a trance. It was the first time I noticed that the kids shopping with their mothers looked like me, but didn't dress or sound like me.

As we finished our ice-cream, we headed off and wandered into stores. My mother was just elated that she was surrounded by selection and new fashions. We passed into one store after another. And there it was: a beautiful bubble-gum pink skirt and shirt combo. The outfit looked like it was made for Strawberry Shortcake, with its puffy sleeves, bow tie, white polka dots, and grosgrain ribbon all over it. It was everything glorious about 80's fashion. I was totally and utterly in love. My mother was in a state of shock. I had only ever worn my grey uniform skirt; getting me into a skirt or dress was like watching what a cat does when you put them anywhere near water. I was allergic to the idea of wearing anything that required me to be polite and didn't fall over my head showing my panties while practicing cartwheels.

So there my mother was, standing in the middle of JC Penney, with a kid who had been dragged on a car ride disguised as a vacation, looking at a ghastly outfit...what did she do? She bought it for me. I was thrilled! I already had it in my head that I would wear it on my first day to my new school, because there was no uniform, and everyone would love me in my pink outfit.

My mother stopped to buy herself a couple of things, but I don't remember what they were, because I had gotten something far grander.

By the time we got back to the hotel, my father was sitting outside, enjoying his book, and smoking his pipe. I guess I forgot to mention: my father was a pipe smoker, he always looked rather dashing and sophisticated smoking his pipe.

He looked at our shopping bags, slightly amused, and asked what we had bought. I told him I would put on a fashion show for him. I raced into the room and quickly put on the outfit, bow tie and all, and pranced out.

I still remember my father's reaction; he did a very good "beautiful" for me, with a big hug. Years later he told me there had not been enough diplomatic training in the world to disguise his laughter. He said it was just about the ghastliest outfit he had ever seen. My mother said it was hard to persuade me that it wasn't beautiful, but she bought it for me anyway. I think it was to make up for the fact that this road trip was a horrid idea.

The car got fixed, and we were back on the road, me in the back, sweaty in a sea of pillows and blankets, holding on to my new outfit like it was my precious. By then, my mother started giving me chocolate and candy from gas stations, keeping me semi-awake between Gravol and sugar. All the cities we passed blurred. We didn't stop for major sightseeing, because sightseeing would be too random for my father; he kept to a military-like schedule. I couldn't figure out why you would bother going on a road trip if you weren't going to stop and enjoy stuff along the way, but it did turn out, my father was trying to gun it faster to Ottawa. Apparently, the furniture which had been in storage for six years had a slightly early release. My father was not impressed. If we didn't make it to Ottawa, the container would be sitting in our driveway without us.

I kept asking, "Are we there yet?" My father started to snap, "We will get there when we get there." Ugh, it was starting to feel like punishment. There was no vacation in this equation.

When we finally got to the Canadian border, my father's

grin was so big. My mother almost leapt out of the car and raced to the Canadian side. The diplomatic passports were handed over, and the border control officer said, "Welcome home." I remember distinctly asking, "Why did he say that?" This wasn't home.

My father tried explaining we were in Canada now, and we were home, but the point was utterly lost on me. Home at that time was a house in Mexico.

There we were, bumping through Montreal, trying to get to Ottawa as quickly as possible. We pulled up to the house my parents had bought nine years before. My great-aunt and uncle were standing there, with our happy dog so beyond excited to be reunited with us that she kept peeing everywhere. I had never met my great-aunt or uncle, they were new to me, but it was obvious that from the tears of joy my mother was shedding while hugging them, they were pretty important to her. She was home. She felt completely relaxed and at ease. I was not; this was all new, and foreign. My father, on the other hand, was already tense, feeling pressure. The moment we moved back to Ottawa, he was waiting and working towards the next move, the next adventure. My mother just wanted to sleep, unpack, and be surrounded by everything familiar for a while. But honestly, the moment my father announced a posting, my mother would dive back into the world of packing, moving, unpacking, learning a new language, settling in, then packing, moving, and unpacking again.

Home to us was wherever we planted ourselves for three years.

29

AN UNEXPECTED FRIENDSHIP -
LISA WEBB

As an avid traveller, I've certainly experienced culture shock that's stopped me in my tracks. Like the time in Peru, when chickens ran round my feet in a one-room, dirt-floor home, as a generous local family served me one of their prized flock for dinner. I worried I would be sick - and I was - but somehow that has made the boldest of memories even more potent. Or the time in India when I was in a taxi and street kids were tapping on the window, begging with such desperation in their eyes that I felt simultaneously grateful and guilty simply for being born where I was. When we found out we were moving to Congo I kept moments like these in the back of my mind. I had no idea what was in store since I hadn't visited the country before we arrived there to take up residency, with all of our belongings, and our two very young children. I expected the worst, but hoped for the best. Had I not had some of my prior travel experiences, landing in the new country I'd call 'home' may not have been so easy. Don't get me wrong, there is a level of poverty in Congo that I wish did not exist in the world. I regularly had waves of guilt for being one of the *haves*, because the *have-nots*, well, I probably don't even know the half of it.

Yet, it's amazing what a person can get used to, because for the most part, during my two years in Congo, I didn't have any culture shock at all. I'd see things that upset me, and I have heard stories about local kids that are enough the break the hardest of hearts, but I never really felt *shocked* by the culture because I had travelled to developing countries before.

Except for one thing: the gap.

The gap between the *haves* and the *have-nots* is something that was in my face daily. I'm slightly uncomfortable even writing about it because by acknowledging it, I'm admitting that I was aware; that I saw it. But how could I not, when I lived it.

I will be the first to admit that I didn't even know just *how* good I had it. I complained, more than once, about life in Congo while I was there. Yet, there are people there who would have given *anything* to trade places with me; to live in the apartment that I found *too small* and *too old*. We tried to help out where we could while we were there: volunteering, donating, hiring a local cleaner and driver, helping them and their families however we could.

Without intention, our cleaner, the Congolese person I knew best, *became* my culture shock. Not because of anything specific she did, but simply because of the insight I got into her life over the years. It left me with a shocking realization of how much I take for granted in my own life.

We'd learned from our time in Indonesia that employing

domestic staff is not a simple case of becoming *those* people, too privileged to do our own housework. We had found ourselves responsible for the livelihoods of a whole group of people, and their extended families. When we arrived there, we agreed to take over the domestic help of the family whose house we were moving into, but quickly found ourselves in a situation where we inherited an employee we felt we had to keep on, because firing them would have been too guilt-inducing.

So when we got to Congo I was no longer a rookie. I knew that we'd hire local help, but this time, I was committed to meeting the person who would be spending the days in our house first, before I hired them. It seems obvious, I know, but it's quite common for expats within the same company to just take over from the family before them.

After about a week in my new location I was starting to feel settled in; after all, this was my third country in three years. The kids were off to school and I jumped right into the international community and joined the monthly coffee morning. I was quickly in my comfort zone, surrounded by a group of diverse women from more nationalities than I could keep track of, welcoming me. It was my happy place!

We got to chatting about how I was adjusting. "The only piece still missing is finding a *ménagère*," I reported, already using the local word for a nanny or cleaner.

I explained that a few of the other *ménagères* on the compound had knocked on the door when they heard there was a new family, to see if their '*soeur*' could stop by to be interviewed for the job. In Congo, everyone is a 'sister'. *Soeur* is a term of endearment for a close friend, but it gets confusing to tell when someone is *actually* a sibling.

"I might have someone for you," Carrie, the American woman who was hosting the coffee morning, offered. "She's actually in the kitchen right now if you want to go meet her."

She was the niece of Carrie's *ménagère* and she often came over to help when there were big groups of people, like for parties or coffee mornings.

"I'll pretend I'm looking for a glass!" I announced, keen to sneak a peek at my possible new house help.

It was a feeble attempt to be subtle because this coffee morning was running like a well-oiled, catered event with clean glasses lined up neatly on the sideboard, but I strolled into the kitchen and offered a *bonjour* and a smile.

At the kitchen sink, elbows deep in soapy water, was a young woman with thick, pink braids down to her waist. She turned around at my *bonjour* and flashed me a huge, warm, genuine smile. She could have been Congolese Barbie. We got to chatting a bit and she didn't stop smiling at me as she navigated my imperfect French, since she didn't speak a word of English. When I thought her smile couldn't get any bigger, she proved me wrong when I asked if she would be interested in coming to do a trial week working at my house.

She eagerly accepted with a, "Oui, Madame!" And the rest is history.

Merveille worked for us for two years and became much more than our cleaner. I'm not sure who learned more: her from me, or me from her.

One day, early on in her time with us I walked into the kitchen to find her eating the leftovers on the kids' plates. I felt instant guilt for our *laissez faire* waste. She blushed for a moment when she saw me, then shyly told me in French that I was a good cook. On the spot we made a new house rule that all leftovers were packed up and she was to take them home to her family, since my own family was slightly spoiled and not big on leftovers. We learned to not over-fill our plates, instead going back for a second helping if we wanted more, so that nothing was thrown out. And I mean *nothing*.

"Madame, you should use the tomatoes this weekend, they're going to go bad," she'd tell me.

"Take them," I'd reply, knowing that going out to eat on the weekends was something we looked forward to in Congo, and I wouldn't be cooking with them before they went bad. In two years not a scrap of food went in the garbage and we all felt good about that.

About a month or two before Christmas in Merveille's first year with us, she asked if we would give her a small loan to buy a computer. This is something common between expats and their domestic help. She knew we were going to France and asked if I would buy her a modest laptop. She proposed to pay us back by having us withhold a small portion of her pay over the course of several months; kind of like a cash advance with a payment plan. I knew this was the only way she could ever afford a computer, and her Christmas bonus alone could cover the cost, so I agreed without hesitation.

She was thrilled when her laptop arrived.

In private, my husband asked me if I thought she would know how to use it. He wanted to make sure she could install the software and set everything up, but he didn't want to offend her if that was too simple a task. We really didn't have a clue of her technological capabilities.

As we were showing her the laptop, Kevin, using his kindest voice, not wanting to offend, asked if she knew how to install the software.

The answer was no. Not a problem, he would do it for her. I could see his thought process continuing without him even saying anything. He was wondering how much she actually knew about computers and what she would use this one for. We knew first hand that internet access in Congo was a luxury.

His next question: *Do you know anyone who has internet you'll be able to use?*

The answer was again no. At this point my culture shock was setting in. Merveille was a single mom in her mid-twenties and I understood that she likely would not have internet access at home because we, as *haves,* paid an extortionate amount each month to stay connected with loved ones and Netflix. But the fact of not even knowing anyone who had internet access quickly shed a bright light on the reality of the situation.

The next question, after an appropriate amount of chitchat, so she didn't feel badgered, was, *Have you ever used a computer?*

The answer was no, and my mind was blown.

I felt privileged. Embarrassed. Sad. Angry. I felt 100% in culture shock.

As an educator, I have witnessed a classroom full of kindergarten kids operate Smart boards. As a parent, I've watched my three-year-old Skype her cousins and my five-year-old FaceTime her grandparents. When I was a teenager, my generation pioneered the internet. I often marvel at the fact that my children have never known life without it. Especially having always lived on the other side of the world and using it almost daily to communicate with family. I've heard of a lot of things, but that was the first time I'd heard of a twentysomething never having used a computer. Gobsmacked: there's no other word for the reaction I was trying to hide.

"You'll learn tomorrow," I told her, hoping that teaching her computer mastery would wash away some of the guilt and embarrassment I was feeling for having cluelessly spent my days beside her, typing on, chatting through, and effortlessly navigating something that I never even realized was a privilege.

The next day cleaning was set aside and we spent the day learning how to use a laptop. Soon after we found a basic computer course in town that we signed her up for. She learned to type, use Word and do basic secretarial work. We thought that, in the worst-case scenario, if there was no other family for her to work for once we moved, she would always have the possibility of getting an office job.

I joked that she'd better not take her new education and leave us for a better job.

"*Jamais Madame!*" She promised that would never happen, adding her huge smile for good measure, and confirming that we were now starting to get each other's sense of humour.

Life in Congo could get lonely at times because there wasn't much to do, but I never really felt *alone* because

Merveille would always be in the house. There were definitely times when I *wanted* to be alone, of course. Some days I missed being able to stroll down the hallway in my underwear. But for the most part, I really started to enjoy her company. I'm not sure when exactly it happened but we developed a friendship of sorts after spending so much time together.

"Madame, you're getting too skinny, stop exercising!" she'd jokingly scold me, as she'd walk in and see me on the spin bike in the living room.

Then she'd tell me I looked much better after we'd return from vacation, where I'd somehow always gain five to seven pounds in a matter of weeks from overindulging. She taught me that in her culture curves are better, and the fact that I was trying to *lose* weight was shocking to her.

In our second year in Congo I asked her to stay late one weeknight because the international community was having a quiz night at one of the local bars. She liked when we'd have her babysit 'after hours' because it meant extra spending money for her, and since she lived with her parents they would watch her daughter. Sometimes she'd joke, "You should go out this weekend," then laugh to herself, and I knew it was because she wanted babysitting money and usually, my arm didn't have to be twisted to make an impromptu date night with Kevin.

The evening of the quiz night, Kevin was running late and I was starting to get slightly irritated that everyone would be waiting for us at the bar. I was ready to go, tapping my toes at the kitchen table when he walked in, not looking so great.

"Sorry I didn't get a chance to call. I don't think I'm gonna go tonight. I don't feel well."

Not doing my best job at hiding my impatience about being late, I told him I hoped he felt better and I was going to go right away before it started.

Kevin turned to Merveille and thanked her for staying, but explained that we wouldn't need her to babysit since he wasn't going out.

The next day she started a conversation that I could tell she was approaching with caution.

"Was Monsieur angry last night?" she inquired.

"Him? No, he wasn't angry. *I* was angry that he made me late. Why would *he* be angry?"

"You went out without him," and after a moment's hesitation she added, "Here, a man would hit you." Another pause. "He didn't hit you?"

She must have seen my jaw sag wide open.

"Never." I said, in a more serious tone than she'd probably ever heard me use.

I took this as an opportunity to explain the way we, as Canadians, view this subject. I told her that no matter what I ever did, it would *never* be okay for Kevin, or anyone, to hit me; that he never would, and if he did, he could go to jail.

Now it was her turn to look shocked.

Our relationship continued like this over the years. Merveille was still our house helper who would clean for us, and watch the kids when we needed her to, but little by little she'd also start giving me advice on which shoes looked better with my outfit, she'd paint her nails with me on babysitting nights before I went out, and zipped my dress up in the back if Kevin was in the shower. I'd ask her about life in her village, Congolese cooking, and learned all sorts of fascinating facts about African woman and their hair-culture...like the fact that a weave should be tapped, not scratched.

While I was packing to move near the end of our time, she shyly inquired about the Ziplock bag full of Tampons under my bathroom sink, that I'd imported from France. They didn't sell them in Congo so I made sure I was well stocked. In hindsight I wonder for how long she had wanted to ask me, since she waited until almost the last possible moment.

I told her it was for *that* time of the month. She replied that she knew that part, which made sense since she did clean my bathroom on a daily basis for two years. But she wanted to know how it was used. I paused for a moment, unprepared for this conversation. Since my own girls were only four and six years old, I figured I had a few years before I needed to broach this subject.

I stumbled over my French for a few minutes, since this is a conversation I never imagined having, let alone in my second language, then, without overthinking it, I reached for a tampon and ripped open the package. I was fully clothed, but found myself suddenly acting out a scene of menstrua-tion charades with my Congolese cleaner.

"Tu comprends?" I double-checked that she understood and she nodded yes, and asked if she could have them. We both laughed and I said of course, but warned her that it would be hard to go back once she ran out. I couldn't even specify what she would be going back to, because I had no

idea. I just knew that from what I saw in the local stores, it wasn't 'Tampax Sport variety pack' quality.

The rest of the packing to move was bittersweet. Merveille could see I was having trouble fitting everything in and would joke, "You don't have room for those purses, just leave them here," and burst into laughter, knowing full well if I left them, they'd be gifted to her and she'd be thrilled. We had already filled our SUV with the contents of our play-room, and driven the pink equivalent of Toys R Us out to her village for her daughter and the other kids in her extended family.

Luck was on her side, because in true mom-fashion, in those final days, I packed the entire house and left my things until the end. We were at maximum capacity, and the airline knew that anyone flying from Pointe-Noire to Paris was one of the haves, slapping high charges on extra baggage. I was already at 14 suitcases and my closet was still full. I took a few necessary items, and, with a deep breath, told Merveille that the entire contents of my closet now belonged to her.

"But wait until I'm gone to take it, I can't watch." I was only half joking because it really would sting to watch my clothes walk away.

"*Vraiment?*" She double-checked that I was serious about giving her my closet, and when I nodded she broke out into a rhythmic happy dance on the spot, as only a Congolese woman could, whooping and hollering in my bedroom like she'd just won the lottery. Then she wrapped me up in a huge hug, trying unsuccessfully to have me join her in danc-ing, but my hips were born in the wrong hemisphere to be able to move like that.

"Share it with your sisters," I told her with a smile, feeling proud of myself for now knowing the local lingo.

Somewhere along the way, on a trip back to France, we brought her back a phone and found a more cost-effective internet source for mobile phones. Merveille downloaded WhatsApp and that became the way she'd get in touch with us for babysitting, or just general communication. She changed her profile picture on there with a greater frequency than social media influencers post on Instagram. Most photos were selfies, and almost all of them took place in our house, since even though we saw it in the light of a university dorm, it was considered luxurious by local standards, and perfect for her selfie backdrops. I'm not sure if she didn't realise we could see her profile pictures of her in our en suite, or if she just didn't care, but it became a little inside joke between Kevin and I when she'd message us.

Now that we're back in Canada we still hear from Merveille regularly. We don't video call because we don't want to use up all her mobile data, but she sends voice memos and is always asking for me to send pictures of the girls and telling us that she loves and misses us. She says her new employer is 'nice' but she's no *Madame Lisa!*

There's been more than once that I've felt annoyed while getting ready for work or to go out because my favourite dress, belt, purse, or shoes that I'm looking for was left in Congo. But then I'll get a message from Merveille and see her profile picture, with her smiling proudly while wearing my entire wardrobe from hat to shoes and everything in between, with a littering of my kids' old toys behind her in the background, and I can't help but smile. My things are far more appreciated in her closet than they would be in mine.

I never expected to have our housekeeper become so close. It was most definitely an unlikely friendship. But making friends with someone of a different age, language, culture, and socio-economic place in the world, offers a powerful potential for learning. I can now see my life as one of privilege simply because of where I was born, and the fact that as a culture, we take things like water and basic education for granted. I cringe now if I have to throw out food, and think of the help we've had along the way with great appreciation, every time I see the laundry baskets in our house overflowing.

As for Merveille, I hope she's learned something from me as well, and that she'll use the relationship Kevin and I have, to which she had a front row seat for two years, as an example of how things can be. We aren't perfect, but I do think that our cultural standards on equality and how to treat each other are healthy.

Merveille tells me on our WhatsApp chats that she hopes to come to Canada and visit one day. I know it's not that simple because of her daughter, finances, visas, and miles of red tape.

But if it's ever possible, we'll be at the airport with open arms, waiting for her to appear wearing all of my favourite clothes.

ACKNOWLEDGMENTS

Thank you to the women who have come forward with their stories of international life. You are the soul of this book, and through these pages you're helping others who might be wondering 'what if' about life on the move. I wouldn't have been able to put this book together without the help of my amazing copy-editor, Catriona Turner. She has been my expat-sister, work partner, and friend through several international moves, and still, she always knows where to put the commas.

And last, but certainly not least, I need to once again thank my family. It's not surprising that this book was born as a coping mechanism while I found my feet through another international move. You've been supportive, as always, as I threw myself into the words on my laptop as literary therapy. Thanks for understanding that writing keeps me sane!

CONTRIBUTING AUTHORS

Nicola Beach

Nicola Beach is a second-generation expat, who grew up in the UK, the Netherlands and Thailand. Her eclectic career history includes forays into direct marketing, customer relations, then a switch to finance. Since 2004 she has been an expat spouse, (or to quote her husband an 'expensive habit'). During this time she has dodged bullets in Lagos and stray cats in Istanbul, before getting cosy in Jozi (Johannesburg) and is currently living the highlife in Hong Kong. Along the way, this globetrotting Brit and Jill-of-all-trades has wrangled her two growing children and acquired a portfolio of strange and useful skills and languages, learned to work with precious metals and gems at jewellery school and moonlighted as a theatre critic. She writes about her family's far-flung adventures at expatorama.com or you can follow her on Facebook @Expatorama. She was previously published in the *Knocked up Abroad Again* anthology.

Helene Benoit

Helene Benoit grew up in a bilingual/cultural family in Norway. She has been traveling the world since 2001, when her French oilman in blue coveralls whisked her away. While this is the first time any of her work is being published, she has been contemplating the social world around her through her cultural glasses, shaped by a masters degree in social anthropology. Her journey has taken her from a pre-Arabic Spring Tunisia, to an economically booming Brazil (where the family grew from two to four), a stop in a disorganized Angola, followed by three long winters in Siberia, then 5 content years in the heart of consumer society, Texas, to finally find herself in Congo, the land of intermittent electricity and eternal summer. She's starting to see the end of her expat story, and somewhere inside there's a voice whispering: *it's too soon*. Writing for *Life on the Move* has given her a taste for writing, so keep your eye out for more.

Robin Blanc

Born in the snowy Midwest, Robin is an ATCK who grew up enjoying the beaches and sunshine in the Bahamas. She has traveled for fun, and studied overseas in Canada, Brazil, Austria, and South Africa. After teaching ESL in Japan and China, she is currently living in Korea and working with university students. You can follow her adventures on her blog robinstl.wordpress.com.

Diana Bond

Growing up in rural Alberta, Diana was 14 before she

saw the ocean for the first time – and was hooked. After obtaining her nursing degree, she spent six months backpacking Australia and New Zealand. She then explored working options and found herself in Riyadh, Saudi Arabia where she met and married her British husband. Life then took them to Japan, Turkey, Korea, Hong Kong, Thailand and finally Australia, which is now 'home'. Along the way they experienced the highs and lows of raising third culture kids and are the proud parents of three amazing multicultural young adults. Her own experience with infant loss influenced her work in perinatal research. Diana is currently enrolled as a PhD candidate at the University of Sydney. Having published extensively in medical journals in the past 10 years, she is thrilled to be publishing from a more personal perspective.

Chantalle Bourque

Chantalle grew up on Canada's east coast before heading west to start her teaching career. Her first foray into a world of globetrotting was as a teacher onboard Class Afloat – a high school on a tall ship. The experience was a lesson in travel's unrivaled ability to teach and be a launchpad for growth and reflection. Enamored with the perspective shift that being in a foreign land allows for, Chantalle explored international teaching opportunities, landing in Abu Dhabi for a few years. She has since returned to Calgary, where she develops travel options for her high school students, and facilitates their exchange options abroad. You can find snapshots of her adventures by following her on Instagram @chant_b, and read her reflections on mylifeasatraveling teacher.blogspot.com.

Margo Catts

Margo Catts grew up in a homebody house in Los Angeles, reading stories from places she hadn't seen and imagining life in all of them. After raising children from east to west in the U.S., she and her husband finally got onto the international circuit, traveling whenever possible and eventually moving to Saudi Arabia, and they are now eyeing an international retirement. She enjoys cycling, which makes her hungry, and cooking, which calls for more cycling, and enjoying both when she travels. Her first novel, *Among the Lesser Gods*, was published by Arcade Publishing in 2017. She currently lives in Houston, Texas, where she is at work on her second. Visit her website margocatts.com to learn more about the books and to follow her blog. You can also follow her author page on Facebook, and find her on Twitter @margocatts.

Lucy Chow

Lucy Chow wants to live in a world where students can come up with the next start-up Unicorn, because she is passionate about innovative businesses. As a Canadian expat, she has been fortunate to have lived in Shanghai, HongKong, New York and most recently Dubai. Unfortunately, out of all those countries, she only picked up the language of natives from New York. (She can do a broad New Yorker accent like nobody's business!) Her contribution to *Life on the Move* is her first published piece in a book, but hopefully not the last!

Follow her on Instagram @lucy_connector, LinkedIn and Facebook @lucy.chow.10.

Cecile Dash

Cecile Dash was born in The Netherlands, married a Canadian backpacker that she found in London and is a mom of three beautiful little monsters (oops meant to write children). Taking care of others is her second nature and when moving from The Netherlands to Congo this was something, she applied wherever she went. Falling in love with Congo and its people made it even harder to leave after 5 years. She currently lives in Dubai and the contrast is big #fromjungletodesert. Thinking her family was used to a hot climate after 5 years in Africa she nearly melted during her first Middle Eastern summer. She works as a part-time chauffeur driving her children all over Dubai, attends most of Dubai's infamous ladies' nights and frequent yoga sessions keep her zen. She has the intention of keeping a blog, supermomabroad.com, but never actually writes new stories for it. Cecile has two previously published stories in Knocked up Abroad Again and Once upon an Expat, two more stories are on the way, and if she ever finds the courage, she will publish her first children's book which has been ready for quite some time now.

Kendra Davidson

Born in Ottawa to a Canadian Diplomatic Father. She spent her childhood moving from Canada, China, Mexico, The Philippines, and Venezuela. After a childhood of non stop moving, it made total sense to then work at Foreign

Affairs as an Advisor on a UN file. After years of diplomatic adulating, it was time for a change. She and her husband moved to Vancouver, where they worked in the chaos of the Olympic games, and were just a couple weeks' shy of having an Olympic baby, no one won the office baby watch pool. Like any good adult who has never grown roots, the family had to pack again and move back to Toronto, Ontario with a stint in Montreal in between, where Kendra helped create the Growing Journal as well as started the blog diplomatickid.com, chronicling the funny stories of growing up and working in Foreign Affairs, and the reality of many Diplomatic Kids, not knowing what or where home is. You can follow her on Instagram and Facebook @diplomatickid.

Shannon Day

Shannon Day is co-author of the book *Martinis & Motherhood: Tales of Wonder, Woe, & WTF?!*, a collection of funny and heartwarming stories (plus easy-to-make martinis) for moms. Shannon lives in the Toronto area with her British husband and their three daughters. Her writing can be found at several online sites including BLUNTmoms, where her story in this book was originally published. Connect with Shannon on Facebook and Twitter @martinisandmotherhood.

Stephanie Lorraine Duncan

Stephanie Lorraine Duncan is an elementary school teacher, a freelance writer and a mother of three living in Toronto, Canada. Before her little ones took over her life, she travelled extensively to every corner of the globe, living and teaching in England, Thailand and Australia. She refuses to give up her love of traveling so nowadays she can be found jet setting with three young children in tow (yes, she's that woman at the airport!). Stephanie fell in love with the people and culture of Thailand when she lived there, and it is these fond memories which are chronicled in this book. She hopes to one day return with her family to the country that stole her heart and taught her how to find her inner peace.

Stephanie's stories have been published in Huffington Post Canada, ScaryMommy, CafeMom and in Vitalize Magazine. Her blog, survivinglifedaily.com, is a realistic and humorous take on how to survive frantic daily life. You can follow Stephanie Lorraine Duncan on Facebook, Instagram and Twitter @survivinglifedaily.

Marcey Louise Heschel

Marcey Louise Heschel is a Canadian mental health therapist, writer, mother and wife. Through her husband's career in oil and gas she has had the opportunity to live and work abroad in both Texas and Malaysia. Although currently repatriated into Canada, she looks forward to her family's next overseas adventure. Marcey spends her days as a stay at home mother and runs a private in person and online therapy practice, Mojo Counselling, on evenings and weekends. Her passions include helping others help themselves, half marathon running and shipwreck diving. If she could be found in her element it would either be diving tropical reefs near a white sand beach or snowed in and cuddled up sipping a fine red wine in a Northern Canadian log cabin. She believes that authenticity and vulnerability are two of the most admirable human characteristics and she seeks to bring that message to others through her lifestyle, work and her writing. Marcey has been published in Once Upon an Expat and Knocked up Abroad Again. She holds a Bachelor's degree in Anthropology and English as well as a Master's degree in Counselling. She is currently pursuing registration as a Psychologist and believes that her education and travels have created a professional niche for her in working with and understanding people of varying cultures and ethnicities. Find Marcey on Instagram, Facebook, LinkedIn, Twitter @mojocounselling and her website mojocounselling.ca.

Sandra Glueck-Taglieber

Born and raised in Austria, Sandra Glueck-Taglieber met her other half right after graduating from University and accompanied her boyfriend and later husband to his postings in the United Arab Emirates, Croatia and Canada. After heading the marketing for the cargo division of the national airline based in Abu Dhabi, founding a local subsidiary of an Austrian head-hunting company in Zagreb, and starting her portable career in "storytelling" in Montreal, Sandra now is a proud mom/preneur who loves to draft and shape concepts and to match words and pictures to bring across ideas. She also is a co-founder of VIE LESA, a non-profit association for Expat Partners in Vienna, who helps them to re-build their lives and careers and speaks up for Dual Careers in Austria.

Amanda Hein

Amanda grew up in small town Ontario and often dreamed of exploring the world. She made her dream a reality in 2010 when she left Canada to teach English in South Korea for a year. From then, she was hooked and wanted to explore as much as the world as possible. In 2013 she moved her life again overseas but this time to Germany where she has been ever since. She recently began writing about her experiences living away on her blog, canadianingermany.com and can be found on Instagram @life_is_an_abenteuer sharing many of her travel photos and life.

Nina Hobson

Nina's topsy turvy expat life is a veritable treasure chest of hilarious, startling and at times terrifying anecdotes. From beach-side parties with diamond merchants, arms dealers and aid workers in Angola, to studies at an ultra-conservative mosque in Syria, and bureaucratic ridiculousness in Switzerland, Nina's expat life has been quite an adventure. Now based in Santiago de Chile, Nina is chronicling her journeys on her popular blog, theexpater.com. In addition to a slice of her latino life, The Expater offers tips and interviews with experts on beauty, travel, well being, parenting and all things expat lifestyle. Follow her on Instagram, Facebook and Twitter @theexpater, and check out her most recent project, The International Women's Club, a new digital platform connecting and inspiring women globally.

Ashly Jeandel

Born in the heart of Canada, Ashly Jeandel grew up in the small town of Erickson, Manitoba. After a year-long backpacking trip around the world she decided to settle in the small French village of Ventron, tucked away in the rolling mountains in Eastern France. When working as an au pair she met her future husband and they decided to put down roots in the small French ski village. She is now married, has two children and runs her own successful business as an English consultant and teacher (clareellaconsulting.com). Ashly has been previously published in Once Upon an Expat and enjoys writing and traveling in her free time.

Mondi Gale Karvouniaris

Mondi Gale is a widow, mother, and writer. In 2015 she tragically lost the love of her life in their home country of South Africa. She survived by travelling with her newborn daughter, who had been on more than 30 flights by the age of three, and by finding solace in the written word. Her late husband, Costa, had wanted so much more for his family and, to honour his memory, his desire for a safer home, and their combined love of travel, she decided that she wanted a better life for herself and their beautiful daughter. So in 2018, Mondi Gale moved halfway across the world with her daughter and mother to Canada. Determined to find the beauty in the world again she found a new home near the mountains in Alberta where she continues to write. Her hope is that in sharing her journey she can inspire and encourage other women to have courage and realize the magnitude of their inner strength. Become a part of Mondi's story at iamthewim.com or follow her on Instagram @iamthewim and remember that no matter what happens in life you can make your own happiness.

Erica Lewindowski

Erica is a mom of two who was a full-time commercial banker in her former life. Struggling daily with the task of keeping the 'mom guilt' at bay when her kids were young, Erica and her family didn't hesitate when the opportunity presented itself to move overseas and start a new adventure together. For the next five years they lived in the south of France, enjoying family time, experiencing the culture, learning the language, and realizing that the road to happiness can be the very same one you thought you were lost on. Erica has since repatriated to Florida and is in the process of finding her new road to happiness. Let the adventures continue... no matter where you find them.

Jasmine Mah-Innocenti

Jasmine grew up a second-generation Canadian on the Western part of Canada in Edmonton, Alberta. She studied Italian and Pharmacy at the University of Alberta and thoroughly enjoyed her community pharmacy practice after graduating in 2013. She was a practicing pharmacist for just more than one year prior to packing her bags for Italy where she now resides. Jasmine founded her award-winning lifestyle blog questadolcevita.com in 2014 and has been featured in Italian newspapers Corriere della Sera and BergamoPost. In addition to blogging, she has been an English consultant to marketing and sales teams in the cosmetics and cosmetics packaging industry, an Italian-English translator, and a freelance travel writer specializing in Italian destinations, food, and culture. She is passionate about reading, writing, food, wine, travel, and cats.

Lasairiona McMaster

Lasairiona McMaster grew up dreaming of an exciting life abroad and after graduating from Queens University, Belfast, that is exactly what she did – with her then-boyfriend, now husband of almost ten years. Having recently repatriated to Northern Ireland after a decade abroad spanned over two countries (seven and a half years in America and eighteen months in India), she now finds herself 'home', with itchy feet and dreams of her next expatriation. With a penchant for both travelling, and writing, she started a blog, lasandcolgotexan.com during her first relocation to Houston, Texas and, since repatriating to Northern Ireland, has decided to do as everyone has been telling her to do for years, and finally pen a book (or two) and get published while she tries to adjust to the people and place she left ten years ago, where nothing looks the same as it did when she left. Follow her on social media @Queenoffirelas.

Akajiulonna Patricia Ndefo

Akajiulonna Patricia Ndefo, born and raised in Lagos, Nigeria, is a wife and mom of three third-culture children. Having bid goodbye (for now) to geosciences, Akaji or Patricia to her family and friends, has over the years made a home in The Netherlands, France, Canada and now in the USA. While on the move she dabbled into global HR, some banking and even modelling for Adoniaa Beauty Inc. However, in all these career changes, writing has been a constant, now her second published writing while embracing expatriate living. Her first was featured in the anthology *Once Upon An Expat*. Patricia enjoys reading, writing, watching soccer, playing board games and hanging out with her lady friends.

Gabriela O'Malley

Passionate about keeping life moving forward and knowing something about change and transitions, Gabriela founded EnRoute.Life – a learning and development coaching and consulting company from Palo Alto, CA to support people in transition in creating strategies for personal and professional development. She's a Career Coach and Consultant at NetExpat – a global leader in expat partner assistance, where she specializes in helping her expat clients build portable careers and achieve their professional goals. Gabriela lived in Mexico and England before she met her husband. For the next fifteen years, they ventured through Germany, Singapore, Spain and a few states in the US; successfully keeping their family in one piece through nine relocations and 11 homes. Wife, mom and writer. Her essays on life, changes, transitions and relocation can be found at NetExpat's Expat Life Blogs and her website enroute.life.

Shirley Prevost

Shirley is an extremely positive and motivated person. She did not hesitate to quit her career as an optician, leave her Canadian home, and to say 'yes' to her husband and allow him to embark upon this opportunity abroad. No u-turns were possible and there have been no regrets!

Shirley lives in Dubai, one of the most futuristic, sparkling, sunny and sandy cities in the world, where camels and Ferraris share the roads.

Shirley and her three children are now as proud to cele-brate UAE National Day as they are to represent Canada at the school International Day.

Between parental obligations, jogging, cooking, and many craft projects, Shirley finds time to write a blog on her experi-ences of living in Dubai and her journey as an expat. You can follow her on Facebook: Shirley: oser la Vie à Dubai.

Melissa Reynolds

Melissa Reynolds is a wife, mother, writer and proud Canadian. She recently left her life in Canada to start a new adventure with her husband and four young children in London, UK. While embracing her new expat life, she still has trouble driving on the other side of the road and has yet to run into Adele to arrange a play date. Pre-children, Melissa was a magazine writer and editor and wrote for many publi-cations and websites. When not shuttling her children around to different activities, Melissa is loving the travel that living in London offers, with the family having explored Amsterdam, Malta, Greece, the Canary Islands, Paris and Scotland already. She also loves reading anything that has words, Netflix, correcting spelling wherever she sees it, looking at artwork, summers back at the family Ontario cottage, going for long walks and the frequent London rain. This is Melissa's first book publication, but you can follow Melissa and her brood's adventures on mumisabroad.wee-bly.com.

Jen Robinson

Jen Robinson, Ph.D. is an Assistant Professor of teaching

English as a second language at Ashford University. She currently lives with her husband and children in the UK. A native of the U.S.A., she enjoys traveling and is thrilled to be a temporary resident of England with dreams of seeing as many countries on that side of the globe as she can. Jen enjoys reading anything and everything, chatting with her children and husband, and learning the intricate nuances of interpersonal communication across the world. You can find Jen on Facebook @jennifer.campbellrobinson, LinkedIn, and at ashford.edu/online-degrees/college-of-education/faculty/jennifer-robinson.

Kimberly Tremblay

Kimberly grew up in St.Albert, Canada where she obtained her B.Ed from the University of Alberta. After teaching for just over a year, she and her husband decided to move to Calgary, Canada where she continued to work as a teacher. Over time she became very interested in the mental well-being of her students and completed a M.Ed in School Counselling. Kimberly then worked as a school counsellor for four years and had two children before moving to Kuala Lumpur, Malaysia. She left Kuala Lumpur two and a half years later for Madrid, Spain where she currently resides. Since moving to Europe with her family, Kimberly has been working as a substitute teacher, travelling and learning Spanish. This is Kimberly's second publication.

Catriona Turner

Catriona is a writer and blogger currently living in Esbjerg, Denmark. In the decade since leaving Scotland, she's also lived in France, Uganda and the Republic of Congo.

On her blog, The Frustrated Nester, she writes about Danish living, travel and the expat life. Her writing has been published in the anthology *Once Upon an Expat*, and she writes a column in *The International*, a magazine for internationals living in Denmark.

She's currently working on a memoir of what home means, and is also a freelance copy-editor and proofreader.

Find Catriona at thefrustratednester.com, and Facebook and Instagram @thefrusteratednester.

Cheryl Walker

With a lifelong love for helping children and a vision for making a difference in the lives of vulnerable families. Montreal native, Cheryl dreamed of working in African communities. When her Congolese husband got a job offer in Congo in 2004, they hardly hesitated. There was a decade of twists and turns, ups and downs, but finally, in June 2014 mwanavillages.org opened its first Mwana Refuge, a holistic orphanage for vulnerable families and children in Congo. Cheryl currently serves as the Director of Operations for the Mwana Refuge and she and her husband Lambert serve on the Board of Directors, overseeing the strategic vision and growth of Mwana Villages.

Lisa Webb

Lisa Webb has been writing as Canadian Expat Mom for many years, across many continents. She's the author of the series, *The Kids Who Travel the World* as well as editor and publisher of the Amazon Bestseller, *Once Upon an Expat.* Lisa is flexing her editing muscles again as she gathers stories from brave and adventurous women across the globe, publishing her second anthology, *Life on the Move.* Follow her adventures on Instagram and Facebook @Canadianexpatmom and her blog canadianexpatmom.com.